Blessings!
Joline
Erlacher

DANIEL
GENERATION

Vigil
Press

SOUTHERN PINES, NC

Daniel Generation is a must read for anyone who wants to meaningfully engage with the next generation and help them rise to the challenge of leading in today's culture. Jolene Cassellius Erlacher expertly weaves together her different experiences in generational trends, student development, and leadership to create a helpful look at the characteristics of our changing culture, the challenges it presents for the next generation, and the unique opportunity for impact it holds. I found this book to be both accurate and honest about the difficulties of our changing culture, and also uplifting and hopeful for the future of the kingdom. I walked away from this book convinced that this next generation is poised to make a monumental impact and I think you will too!

–**Katy White,** Director of Coaching, GoCorps

In a rapidly changing world, we need godly leaders who understand the times, yet are able to lead with integrity and strength. Using the historical account of Daniel, this book provides relevant examples that can be contextualized into current life and culture. Skillfully written and well researched, it offers compelling insights into the Millennials and Generation Z, challenging those from other generations to reconsider how they work with developing leaders. This book is a great resource to begin the process.

–**Camille Bishop,** Assistant Provost for Academic Affairs, University of the Nations

Many lament and despair that America is rejecting its Christian roots. While this is lamentable, Jolene Cassellius Erlacher shows in her recent book that there is a growing cadre of believers who

have found that the success of the Kingdom of God does not rest on historic roots, but on a Daniel-like faith. There is great reason for hope and optimism about the work of God in the world! Thank you, Jolene, for this Bible-based and encouraging message.

–Dr. Gordon Anderson,

former President, North Central University

"(We are) training young leaders today for a world that no longer exists." As one of Jolene Cassellius Erlacher's opening statements, this comment reveals the heart of the problem the church is facing today. The world is changing so rapidly around us – how can we possibly keep up? An expert in generational trends and leadership development, Jolene incorporates relevant research, cultureless/ timeless biblical truth, and practical help to navigate the changing times. Beautifully couched in the godly example of Daniel and his friends in Babylon, Jolene's commitment to the King and his kingdom marinates every morsel of this savory book. She paints a parallel picture of what wise, committed believers need in order to navigate today's American version of Babylon. Whether you are training emerging leaders or are one yourself, read Daniel Generation *and join the remnant God is preparing to hold out hope in the chaos of our times.*

–Carolyn Gabriels, Missionary to Cambodia, World Team

This book takes us on a journey with an Old Testament model of leadership in Babylon. It shows that the Kingdom culture demonstrated by Daniel superseded the culture around him. The timeless principles apply not just in North America, but around the world where leaders are facing their own version of Babylon. Jolene Cassellius Erlacher's call for servant leadership is a must-read for leaders today living in a digitalized world where the pace of change is unprecedented.

—**Bill Mann**, Writer, MentorLink

First Edition, June 2018
Vigil Press
Southern Pines, NC

http://www.leadingtomorrow.org

Editing: Francine Thomas
Publishing and Design Services: Melinda Martin, MelindaMartin.me

ISBN 978-1-7321686-0-2 (print), 978-1-7321686-1-9 (epub)

DANIEL
GENERATION

GODLY LEADERSHIP
IN AN UNGODLY CULTURE

Jolene Cassellius Erlacher

Vigil
Press

SOUTHERN PINES, NC

To Anna and Elizabeth:

May you live as Daniel did—
in God's favor and blessing;
with faith, wisdom, and courage
amid tumultuous times.

CONTENTS

Introduction 1

Part I The World of a Daniel Generation 5

Chapter 1 Our Moment in History 7

Chapter 2 Cultural Earthquake 13

Chapter 3 Judah Has Fallen 25

Chapter 4 Daniel's Challenge 35

Chapter 5 Life in Babylon 45

Chapter 6 God's Heart for Babylon 59

Part II Essential Practices for Leading in Babylon ... 71

Chapter 7 Understanding the Times 73

Chapter 8 Knowing the Law of God 83

Chapter 9 Practicing Discipline 97

Chapter 10 Choosing Godly Companions 109

Chapter 11 Relating to an Ungodly Culture 123

Chapter 12 Serving the King 137

Chapter 13 Living a Trustworthy Life 147

Chapter 14 Seeking Understanding 155

Part III Leadership Perspectives 163

Chapter 15 Leadership Redefined 165

Chapter 16 A Time of Shaking 175

Chapter 17 A Season of a Remnant 185

Resource List 195

Glossary of Terms 197

About the Author 199

Connect with Jolene 200

Acknowledgments

Everywhere I travel, I meet godly young leaders. Some of them are as young as eight or nine; others are approaching middle age. Their passion denotes the same spirit that the queen recognized in Daniel as the "spirit of the holy gods" (Dan. 5:11). Today's young leaders do, in fact, embody the Spirit of the holy God! They inspire, challenge, and encourage me. In writing this, I have often imagined sitting across the table at a coffee shop with one or more of them sharing what God is putting on our hearts for this moment in history. I am deeply grateful for these young men and women who are committed to stand when all others bow to false gods. They will bow only to their God even if it costs them their lives. They are a Daniel Generation!

To everyone who read chapters of the manuscript, asked poignant questions, helped me process my thoughts, gave input, and provided marketing or editing insights, thank you! When I was praying in preparation for this book, I felt God confirm that he was putting together his team for this project. There are too many to mention everyone by name, but know that I am deeply grateful for your valuable assistance and expertise.

A special thank you to Rachel and Francine, my godly companions who journeyed with me during the writing of this book.

This project would not have been possible without the love and support of my husband and children. They continually inspire me as we discover the adventure of living together in the blessing of God. May God grant us the grace, as individuals and a family, to always live godly lives in an ungodly culture.

Introduction

Over the past 15 years, it has been my honor to spend many hours chatting with young leaders in diverse contexts. As I listen to their struggles, questions, and hopes, I realize that they are increasingly faced with decisions and complexities that are unfamiliar and sometimes unrecognized by those of us with years of leadership experience. This is true whether they are on college campuses; working in their local churches, communities, or business; or serving in missions or the military. As a result, I find that many organizations, schools, and ministries are training young leaders for a world that no longer exists. We ask them to "pay their dues" while failing to equip them with the skills they most desperately need to thrive.

As cultural trends show an increasing antagonism toward God, godly leaders face the daunting task of navigating the changing environment. The past experiences of many mentors today differ significantly from those of the young leaders they teach. Today, we are learning to express our faith in a compelling manner on social media, navigate changing views on gender and sexuality, empower ministry outside the church walls, and communicate biblical truth to those who believe Christians are hateful and narrowminded. As a result, this season requires leaders of all ages to discover what it means to be a godly leader in a complex, ungodly culture.

I am convinced that we live in a period of history like that of the prophet Daniel. For many years, we were leaders in our own Judah where our faith harmonized with the culture around us. Now, however, God is calling us to lead in a kind of Babylon where our faith stands in stark contrast to the culture in which we live. This book outlines the challenge of Daniel and his friends, one that reflects the challenge of godly leaders today. Just as the environment of Jerusalem differed from that of Nebuchadnezzar's palace, the context young Christian leaders navigate today is much different than that experienced by their predecessors. We must wrestle with tough questions about what the changes mean for us, for our faith, relationships, and leadership, and for the churches and organizations we serve.

My purpose in writing this book is to offer a tool to facilitate intergenerational understanding and conversation regarding what is required of godly leaders today. Millennial and Generation Z leaders need hope, encouragement, and effective leadership practices for an uncertain future. The story of Daniel, his friends, and their people in exile provide just that. This book examines the life of Daniel and uses it as a template for learning how to thrive in an ungodly context. Despite unbelievable challenges, Daniel earned the favor of those he served, and as a result, was able to influence the most ungodly and powerful individuals of his day. Today, God is calling young leaders to rise to a similar challenge. I pray the following discussion will encourage a generation of Daniels to stand firm in the tumultuous days ahead.

For those of us who had the privilege of leading in the Judah of the past, the question remains, how do we disciple today's Daniels to lead in a context we may never fully understand ourselves? We must learn to embrace new models of mentoring, training, and leadership development. In some cases, it will mean adjusting our expectations or going back to foundational spiritual and leadership disciplines that are becoming increasingly endangered. As we prepare to pass the leadership baton to the next generation, insights from Israel's troubled history will prove invaluable. This is a generation that will see the fourth man in the fire and the angel in the lion's den. As experienced leaders, we must encourage and equip leaders of a new Daniel Generation as they navigate their own season of leadership.

PART I

THE WORLD OF A
DANIEL GENERATION

CHAPTER 1
OUR MOMENT IN HISTORY

A generation which ignores history has no past—and no future.
—Robert A. Heinlein

Some people like surprises. Not me. I am a planner; I want to know what is happening and why. Recently, I experienced a situation at a youth program where I volunteer that produced some angst for my strategy-loving personality. I had taught for years with this same non-profit program. I knew where to find books and paper, who to contact if I was sick and needed a substitute, and the names of my fellow volunteers. I understood our goals and purpose so well that others came to me with questions about planning lessons and managing resources. Serving there felt familiar and fulfilling.

Then, almost overnight, things began to change. New pictures and furniture appeared in my classroom. The paper and books disappeared from their usual location. New volunteers showed up with different ideas about how to run the class I was teaching. I didn't know our purpose anymore and struggled to get clarity on what was expected of me. After years of serving with confidence and passion, I now felt confused and angry. Part of me wanted to just quit.

A new director had taken over the program. New directors bring innovative ideas, different methods, and new people. While often necessary, change can produce frustration when we don't understand what is happening or why. In this case, experienced teachers like me were confused and new volunteers felt frustrated. The newcomers thought we were either refusing or simply failing to do things the correct way. Trained under new guidelines, they knew nothing of the old system or our need to be brought up to speed. As we committed to building a stronger program together, we desperately needed to understand one another in light of what had occurred during the transition of leadership.

Leaders everywhere face situations like that of our volunteer team. A major transition has taken place in our society over the past couple of decades that is resulting in new expectations, values, and norms. As a result, experienced leaders often find themselves struggling to understand how to navigate this new context. Young leaders can feel frustrated and impatient with the failure of their mentors or teachers to understand and adapt to the world as it is. Effective leadership in the days ahead will require us to come together to understand what God is doing in this moment in history.

In the following pages, as we delve into the changes

occurring around us, I hope to encourage a conversation among godly leaders of all ages. I believe this discussion requires an understanding of the current cultural transition and how it impacts our perspectives. Some of us have witnessed the dramatic changes in our world and know all too well the uncertainty that comes with significant upheaval. For others, today's world is all we have ever known. We need insight to understand what is changing and why it matters. The first section of this book will discuss these changes and define the context in which we must lead today.

Our generation is not the first to experience significant change. As historian Peter Drucker explains, "Every few hundred years in Western history there occurs a sharp transformation…society rearranges itself…its worldview; its basic values; its social and political structure; its arts; its key institutions…we are currently living through just such a transformation."[1] Cultural upheavals mark every civilization throughout history. We must, therefore, learn broader lessons from others who navigated their own seasons of change.

To guide our discussion of what godly leadership looks like in an increasingly ungodly culture, we will look at the prophet Daniel who led during an incredibly tumultuous time. Daniel grew up in Judah following the reign of King Josiah. King Josiah had sought to bring the people of Judah back to God, but after his death, the nation continued in their idolatry. Despite many warnings from prophets of God, the people refused to change. As a result, God sent Nebuchadnezzar to invade and conquer Judah. King Nebuchadnezzar took many from Judah into exile in Babylon. It was during this time that Daniel and his young friends were carried into captivity. God granted Daniel favor, and over time, he achieved high status. In doing so, however, he had to learn how to be a godly leader in the context of Nebuchadnezzar's Babylon, a place very different from Judah.

In section two of this book, we will take an in-depth look at the essential leadership practices of Daniel and his friends that allowed them to thrive in an ungodly environment. We will consider what these practices might look like in our own technologically advanced global society, one that David Kinnaman, president of Barna Group, refers to as our "digital Babylon."[2] This section of the book is geared toward Millennial (b.1980-1995) and Generation Z (b. 1996-2012) leaders. The lessons and principles from Daniel's life, however, are applicable to godly leaders regardless of age.

In the concluding section of this book, we will consider what perspectives should inform leadership philosophies and expectations as we look ahead to an unknown future. What does it look like to lead well amid uncertainty and to prepare future leaders for what is to come? How do we position our churches, organizations, communities, and students for what God will do beyond this moment in history?

Daniel and his friends lived during a pivotal time

in the history of God's people. The exile of the Jews in Babylon marked a historical shift that had long-lasting consequences for them and for the world. It is in such critical historical moments like this that God calls on a unique generation of leaders to faithfully stand. I refer to this group as a Daniel Generation. I am convinced this moment in history is one that will mark our world for generations to come. It is time for a new generation of leaders like Daniel to take its place!

Reflections and Applications

What do you see as significant changes and trends in our society today? What is your response to these changes?

What do you think is most critical to effective leadership in times of change and transition? Why?

NOTES

1. Peter Drucker, *Post-Capitalist Society* (New York: Harper Collins, 1993), 1.

2. *Gen Z: The Culture, Beliefs and Motivations Shaping the Next Generation* (Barna and Impact 360 Institute), 2018, 9.

CHAPTER 2
CULTURAL EARTHQUAKE

Culture is the name for what people are interested in, their thoughts,
their models, the books they read...the values they appreciate.
—Walter Lippmann

On most mornings, I wake up feeling compelled to pick up my phone to discover what happened in the world while I slept, to check out what my friends are doing, and connect with others before I start my day. Unfortunately, this is rarely an uplifting exercise. A five-minute review of my news and social media feeds usually reveals yet another corrupt leader, a few more natural disasters, various financial struggles, war, disease, selfishness, anger, and heartache. I seldom put down my phone feeling better about life than I did when I first picked it up!

Technology allows us to see what is happening around the world at any given moment. Much of what we learn is filtered through an endless stream of opinions and emotions. We can't help but feel tension everywhere in our society. Whether people are talking about politics, the economy, relationships, social norms, or their experiences driving to school or work, we sense fear, frustration, anger, and confusion. Our culture is in a state of transition, and the resulting societal earthquake is revealing deep uncertainty, division, and self-interest. As leaders, understanding this context can help prepare us for what we will encounter as we navigate a society in desperate need of hope and purpose.

The 40,000-Foot View

I love flying! Something about seeing the world from 40,000 feet always gives me a distinct perspective on what might otherwise seem like mundane features. From my lofty vantage point, I can see the beautiful patchwork of fields and forget for a moment that they consist of ordinary rocks, dirt, and plants. Even the path of a river seems striking so far above the sound of water lapping at the shore. In much the same way, history gives us an extraordinary 40,000-foot view of culture by providing a broad context for the behaviors, attitudes, and perspectives we see when we're on the ground with only a limited point of view.

Our values—what we believe to be important—provide the foundation for culture. Values determine our moral and ethical standards. One of the most significant changes that can occur in culture is a shift in what we value and how we determine right and wrong. When changes take place in our understanding of morality, the very foundation of societies are shaken. Imagine for a moment the tectonic plates that exist deep below the earth's surface. As they shift, the entire surface of the earth above them does as well. Buildings collapse, chasms open, and the earth's crust is displaced in the resulting earthquake. The landscape after an earthquake can look radically different than before, often requiring significant rebuilding of the areas affected. This is what happens when we redefine the values foundational to how we live and interact with one another. In other words, we experience a cultural earthquake.

A cultural shift of this magnitude occurred about 400 years ago. Historians define the era before the 1600s as the premodern period, a time when most of humanity believed in the divine or supernatural. God, or the supernatural realm, provided the basis for truth, morality, and reason, but that began to change. The seventeenth century produced the rumblings of a massive cultural shift. Beginning with the Renaissance, and reinforced by the Enlightenment and Industrial Revolution, the foundation for how we determined truth changed.

Authors Josh and Sean McDowell explain, "In the Renaissance, man (not God) became central; in the Enlightenment, man's reason became transcendent."[1] They describe how the Industrial Revolution, with its inventions, innovations, and improvements, resulted in men and women witnessing progress all around them. They looked to themselves for hope and guidance instead of seeking God or the supernatural realm for direction. As a society, science and human reason helped us to determine truth. This marked the beginning of the Modern Era, a period of history known for its faith in objective facts, science, and reason.

As humankind approached the twenty-first century, society experienced the throes of yet another seismic change. Postmodern ideas and values quickly overtook the long-treasured values of the Modern Era. Postmodernism, for instance, claims there is no universal foundation for truth or morality. All previously held values, beliefs, and systems are suspect and must be questioned. Our basis for truth moved from God to science, and now to our own preferences and perspectives. This most recent shift is creating a cultural earthquake of immense proportions. Its effects are seen everywhere from social media feeds to international politics, family relationships, and economic developments.

When I consider the trend in our culture toward self-determined truths—choosing to believe what feels good to us in the moment—it occurs to me that we might be practicing the highest form of idolatry. Many other cultures and peoples worshipped false gods and idols over the years, but in most cases, they still bowed, surrendered, and humbled themselves before something they believed to be greater than themselves. Today, we declare ourselves to be the creators of our own truth. In doing so, we make ourselves gods subject to no higher principles, rule, or authority. There is little sense of obligation to a law or rule higher than our own emotions or perspectives.

On the Ground

So, what does this massive cultural change look like in our daily interactions and activities? While there are too many changes to look at them all in detail, let's discuss a few that I consider to be most significant. These impact many of the other behaviors, attitudes, and perspectives representing the shift that has occurred.

Printing Press to Internet

One of the significant factors in the cultural shift from the Premodern to the Modern Era was the invention of the printing press. As the Premodern Era ended, the invention of the printing press by Johannes Gutenberg in the mid-1400s became a catalyst for the Modern Era. In 1455, the initial 200 copies of the Bible were printed and sold to the masses. For the first time, ordinary people had access to the Scriptures as well as to other information fueling growth in science, technology, and scholarship. The information and format of books greatly served to influence our thoughts and behaviors. Researcher Nicholas Carr explains,

> For the last five centuries, ever since Gutenberg's printing press made book

reading a popular pursuit, the linear,
literary mind has been at the center of
art, science, and society. As supple as it
is subtle, it's been the imaginative mind
of the Renaissance, the rational mind of
the Enlightenment, the inventive mind
of the Industrial Revolution, even the
subversive mind of Modernism. It may
soon be yesterday's mind.[2]

Books reinforced the values of the Modern Era. Written in a linear manner with facts and logic to support their claims, they influenced the very way we thought.

In 1991, an invention as significant as the printing press was introduced for the first time. A computer programmer named Tim Berners-Lee unveiled the World Wide Web. This suddenly made the idea of networked computers, a technology that had been around for decades, an accessible reality to ordinary people. With the introduction of the internet, and in 2007, the iPhone, the way we get information, communicate globally, and manage our relationships has been revolutionized. These technological advances influence our knowledge and interactions and, as research now shows, rewire our brains. Nicholas Carr says, "We seem to have arrived at an important juncture in our intellectual and cultural history, a moment of transition between two modes of thinking . . . calm, focused, undistracted, the linear mind is being pushed aside by a new kind of mind that wants to take in and dole out information in short, disjointed and often overlapping bursts—the faster, the better."[3] He explains how our attention spans are shrinking and our ability to think deeply is being threatened. We have developed the ability to skim and sort information at faster speeds. Because we are still on the leading edge of this change, the long-term effects on our minds, relationships, and society are not yet fully understood.

Objectivity to Subjectivity

Another way the cultural shift influences our lives, at least in the short term, is in how we make decisions. During recent presentations on college campuses, I asked students to indicate how they make decisions and whether they base them on facts or emotions. Roughly 80 percent of the students on each campus indicated that they make decisions based on emotion. This represents a shift. In the past, modern thinking taught us to make objective decisions based on what we could prove. We relied on science, facts, logic, and reason to guide us to the best outcome. Postmodern thinking, however, teaches us to make subjective decisions based on what feels right. Today, many of us rely on emotion, story, and experience to determine what is best for our lives.

Predictability to Uncertainty

In periods of cultural stability, we can somewhat accurately predict the outcomes of certain behaviors. For many decades in America, for instance, it was understood that if you worked hard and paid your mortgage and taxes, you could usually count on promotions, raises, a house, and social security or pension. Today, we live in a rapidly changing and unpredictable world. In the past few decades, we have witnessed multiple terrorist attacks and a significant economic recession. We have seen quality employees lose jobs as they neared retirement, hard-working families lose their homes, and big corporations get free passes with government bailouts. Consequences seem unclear and unfair as those who work hard often struggle and those who are corrupt evade punishment. We watch live events around the world 24/7 and fear that anything could happen to us at any time. A sense of uncertainty permeates our view of life and consequently our actions. Fear, skepticism, and living for the moment are common responses to this uncertainty.

Postmodern Natives

I am often asked what is so unique or different about Millennials and Generation Z as compared to older generations. Younger people today are what I like to call *postmodern natives*. They have been raised, educated, and influenced by the emerging culture.

They intuitively understand postmodern values. Even if some are more modern in their thinking, they live in a culture surrounded by peers who are postmodern in their perspectives and actions. Many older adults are also postmodern in their thinking, but they are more likely to have grown up in or been educated according to modern perspectives. As a result, they often retain some of the related views and behaviors. This is frequently at the heart of generational conflict and misunderstandings.

Identity Crisis

As we noted earlier in this chapter, perspectives are changing. Values once held dear are being discarded. Established institutions and methods are being questioned and often rejected. The influences of postmodernism, moral relativism, technology, and globalization are reordering the very foundations of our society. While specifics of all these changes are beyond the scope of this discussion, I recommend several books in the Resource List that further explore the cultural shift we are experiencing.

Amid the ensuing chaos of change, believers today must grapple with significant questions about what we believe and how we will respond to the environment around us. It can feel to some, especially experienced leaders, as if everything they sacrificed and worked for is under attack. Faith-based institutions—from mission agencies, to churches, schools, non-profit organizations, seminaries, businesses, and advocacy groups—are facing an identity crisis. We are being forced to consider how we understand and define truth and how we allow it to inform our decisions and behaviors. All too often we find ourselves caught between those trying to hold onto former methods and views and the overwhelming influence and pressure from our culture that sweeps us toward acceptance of new ideals and perspectives. The pressing question for leaders today is how to negotiate this changing terrain while remaining faithful to who and what God has called us to be. In the next chapter, we will examine more closely the complex cultural landscape that Daniel traversed in his own season of leadership.

Reflections and Applications

Was I raised with a modern or postmodern perspective on the world? What is my perspective today and how has it changed?

How do I define truth? Make decisions? Are my approaches biblically or culturally based?

NOTES

1. Josh McDowell and Sean McDowell, *The Beauty of Intolerance: Setting a Generation Free to Know Truth and Love* (Uhrichsville: Shiloh Run Press, 2016), 61.

2. Nicholas Carr, *The Shallows: What the Internet is Doing to Our Brains* (New York: W.W. Norton & Company, 2011), 10.

3. Nicholas Carr, *The Shallows*, 10.

CHAPTER 3
JUDAH HAS FALLEN

Set your minds on things above, not on earthly things.
—Colossians 3:2

A year ago, I went through a difficult period. I was plagued by anxiety. I struggled to fall asleep, woke up frequently in the night, and developed an ulcer from worrying. The source of my concern? I was stressed about leadership and church-related issues. To make matters worse, I also worried about my business and finances. Important relationships in my life seemed strained and chronic pain from an injury overwhelmed me at times. The angst evident in conversations around me regarding politics, global issues, and injustices only fueled my anxiety. The lens of worry through which I viewed the challenges in my life and the world clouded my understanding.

It is natural in seasons of uncertainty and change to feel anxious, but in my own journey, I am learning that God wants to help his faithful children go beyond what is natural. It does not mean we will not battle those natural feelings, but he wants to give us a perspective that will allow us to lead with courage even in tumultuous times.

During the fall of Judah and the subsequent exile, we see several godly leaders who acted boldly despite their natural fears. They trusted confidently in God's purposes not just for them, but for their people and homeland. Their example can provide powerful inspiration for us today!

The Fall of Judah

Let's look closer at Judah around the year 600 B.C., when Daniel was a boy. The prophets had been warning the people for years that things needed to change. If the people refused to repent, Judah would inevitably fall to her enemies. People could not believe that such a terrible fate awaited them. It seemed impossible! After all, Judah was the place of God's promises as well as their fulfillment. It was the site of the holy city, Jerusalem, and their beloved temple.

Years before, when God led the Jews out of Egypt, he gave them detailed instructions on how to construct a tabernacle in the wilderness. This temporary tent of meeting represented God's desire to dwell among them and to establish his presence with them. Later, after years of waiting and struggle, fighting many battles and experiencing much sacrifice, God allowed his people to build a permanent temple. The temple housed the Ark of the Covenant. It was also the place where the priests offered sacrifices and the high priest went into the holy of holies to meet with God.

The people, however, gradually slipped away from true worship of God. The prophets Jeremiah and Ezekiel exposed idols in the temple of the Lord.[1] They saw that the God of Israel was just one of many gods that the people were worshipping and trying to please. In Jeremiah 44, we see the people's response to the prophet's warning to turn from their worship of other gods: "We will not listen to the message you have spoken to us in the name of the Lord." They defiantly declared, "We will certainly do everything we said we would: We will burn incense to the Queen of Heaven and will pour out drink offerings to her just as we and our ancestors, our kings and our officials did in the towns of Judah and in the streets of Jerusalem."[2] The arrogance of their response is chilling. Yet, as I read this, I am convicted that a similar attitude can exist in my own heart. When do I follow God and his Word unwaveringly versus insisting on doing what I want to do? What do I worship and prioritize above Him?

Judah and her kings refused to listen to the warnings of the prophets as they instructed them to turn from their idolatrous ways. Their disobedience eventually led to the Babylonian invasion and exile that took place between 605-586 B.C. It occurred in three stages with invasions beginning in 605 B.C. when Daniel and his friends were taken to Babylon; in 597 B.C. when King Jehoiakim was taken, and then the final invasion in 586

B.C. when the temple was destroyed. The first chapter of the book of Daniel recounts the initial invasion: "In the third year of the reign of Jehoiakim king of Judah, Nebuchadnezzar king of Babylon came to Jerusalem and besieged it. And the Lord delivered Jehoiakim king of Judah into his hand, along with some of the articles from the temple of God. These he carried off to the temple of his god in Babylonia and put in the treasure house of his god."[3]

This passage clearly shows that the Lord delivered the king of Judah into Nebuchadnezzar's hand and used the evil ruler to do his will. What?!? God's actions must have seemed unthinkable to the people. Not only did Nebuchadnezzar invade, kill, and take away many people, but he also took articles from the temple of God before destroying the temple itself. The devastation the people of God felt when the temple fell is something we cannot comprehend. Its meaning and significance were deeply embedded in their history and culture, yet God wanted their hearts, and in recapturing their hearts, he was willing to strip away everything they worshipped above him. Daniel makes it clear that God was orchestrating this season of shaking in Judah. It was during this time of incredible uncertainty, devastation, and upheaval that Daniel and his friends were called to lead.

Responding to Change

As God's people today who are living in our own period of change, we should feel encouraged. God was not shocked by Nebuchadnezzar's actions, and he is not surprised by the challenges we face. So, if God is leading us through a season of upheaval, what should be our response? In Daniel's day, we see three reactions to what occurred in Judah.

During this time, a number of Jews refused to accept what was happening. They chose, instead, to live in denial. The warning from the prophet in Jeremiah 27 indicated that those who remained in the city of Jerusalem would be destroyed along with the city. I can imagine some clinging to the temple pillars refusing to believe what they had been told. They fell with the temple. This first group was made up of those who chose denial.

The second group can be classified as pouters. They resented the fact that they were in exile. This was not what THEY wanted! Rather than invest their time and energy into making the best of life in a foreign land, they simply wanted to go back home to their comfortable, familiar life in Judah. In Jeremiah 29:4-9, we find God's word to them:

> This is what the Lord Almighty, the
> God of Israel, says to all those I carried
> into exile from Jerusalem to Babylon:

"Build houses and settle down; plant gardens and eat what they produce. Marry and have sons and daughters; find wives for your sons and give your daughters in marriage, so that they too may have sons and daughters. Increase in number there; do not decrease. Also, seek the peace and prosperity of the city to which I have carried you into exile. Pray to the Lord for it, because if it prospers, you too will prosper."

It may come as a shock, but God is not nearly as concerned with our comfort and happiness as we might think. He is much more interested in our obedience and faithfulness to him. His desire to bless us is on his terms, not ours. Those who pouted wanted it their way. God is looking for those who are willing to do it his way.

Daniel and his friends belonged to the faithful, our third group. This group represents those who understood the times in which they lived. They were willing to pursue God's purpose and intentions even it if meant giving up their own rights and comforts. God used this group of people in powerful ways throughout the seasons of exile and the later restoration. Esther, who risked her life to protect the Jews in exile, and Ezra and Nehemiah, the two men who eventually led a number of exiles on a risky adventure to rebuild Jerusalem, are other examples of the faithful few.

So, which group do we belong to? Are we counted

among the deniers who look at the culture today and refuse to accept the changes occurring around us? Are we pouters, willing to serve God only if it involves the comforts, preferences, and views that feel or seem good to us? Or, like Daniel, Jeremiah, Esther, and Ezra, are we willing to accept what God is doing in our day and prepare ourselves to be part of his work? Yes, Judah fell to Nebuchadnezzar, but the purposes of God remained. This is a hope we can cling to regardless of the tumultuous period of history in which we find ourselves.

Things Above

Last year, in my desperate season of anxiety, I cried out to God. Wallowing in fear, I wanted to blame my circumstances, other people, and the crazy world in which we live for my dark thoughts. God gently told me that the source of my anxiety lay in my own disobedience to his Word. In Colossians 3:1-2, Paul writes, "Since, then, you have been raised with Christ, set your hearts on things above, where Christ is, seated at the right hand of God. Set your minds on things above, not on earthly things." When I focused more on my news feed, the opinions of friends on social media, the balance in my bank account, or the pain in my body than on the things of heaven, I could not be effective in serving God and leading others.

Controlling my thoughts was easier said than done. However, my willingness to listen to and obey God set me on a journey toward peace. I found I had to intentionally reinstate certain godly practices into my life and daily routine. As I sought help, God provided the prayer support and counseling I needed. Most importantly, however, I asked God to help me to follow his command to set my mind on things above. I made a list in my journal of those things that are lovely, pure, and right. When I found myself beginning to worry or obsess about earthly things, I intentionally chose to think about those things that were aligned with God's Word. Some days, I failed miserably, and still do, but little by little I began to see the world through a different lens. The hopelessness of this world gave way to the hope of heaven.

A mind set on things above is needed for living as godly leaders in uncertain times. We will understand the importance of this perspective as we continue to discuss the life and leadership of Daniel. A heavenly mindset is something we must actively pursue throughout the changing seasons of our own leadership journey. Only then will we have the right lens through which to address the changes and challenges we face. When we are focused on what God is doing rather than the chaos of the world around us, we will see his perfect purposes accomplished…even if Judah has fallen.

Reflections and Applications

What is my response to the challenges in our culture today? In what ways am I a denier, pouter, or faithful child of God?

How do I respond to anxiety, fear, worry? What is God encouraging me to change in how I view and respond to challenges in my life, my leadership, and the world?

NOTES

1. Jeremiah 32:33-34; Ezekiel 8
2. Jeremiah 44:16-18
3. Daniel 1:3

CHAPTER 4
DANIEL'S CHALLENGE

As you sent me into the world, I have sent them into the world.
—John 17:18

In the classic movie, *The Wizard of Oz*, young Dorothy makes a distressing observation: "Toto, I've a feeling we're not in Kansas anymore!"[1] Indeed, Dorothy and Toto find themselves swept up by a tornado and deposited in the mysterious Land of Oz. They walk on a yellow brick road, talk with Scarecrow, Tin Man, and Cowardly Lion, and join them as companions on their journey to see the great Oz. The Land of Oz proves to be a very different place from Kansas!

Daniel's journey began somewhat like Dorothy's with a dramatic change of scenery. While there were no talking Scarecrows or Tin Men in Babylon, there were golden statues and royal feasts unlike anything in Jerusalem. Daniel and his friends, while living in a lavish and foreign land, provide powerful lessons and encouragement for us today as we find our way through a new cultural and technological landscape far different from any our parents and grandparents experienced.

The Appeal of Babylon

After being taken captive by Nebuchadnezzar's army, young Daniel found himself in the king's palace in Babylon. He had been selected along with other young Jews to take part in a special leadership development program. I can imagine Daniel and his friends, Azariah, Mishael, and Hananiah discussing their surroundings with awe. Daniel may have commented, "Friends, I've a feeling we're not in Judah anymore!"

Historians give us dramatic facts about Nebuchadnezzar's Babylon. The kingdom boasted more than 50 temples (compare that to only one in Jerusalem!), a solid gold image of Baal weighing more than 50,000 pounds, and the famous Hanging Gardens, one of the seven wonders of the ancient world. The Euphrates River ran through the city that was surrounded by two walls, one 25 feet thick and the other 75 feet thick. Nebuchadnezzar's palace, where the Bible tells us young Daniel was taken, was considered to be the most magnificent building on earth. Indeed, the king intended for this experience to be impressive, overwhelming, and life-altering for the young Jews.

Third Culture Kid

The dazzling wealth and power of Babylon were not the only changes Daniel encountered. He found himself in a culture radically different from that of his family back home in Judah. I can imagine a little of how Daniel must have felt. Growing up as a missionary kid in another country, I experienced the tension many third culture kids feel. A third culture kid is someone raised in a culture other than that of their parents for a significant period of their early life. These young people come from one culture, but grow up in another before eventually forming their own culture that often incorporates elements of both.

As a foreigner living in a new place, there is incredible pressure to fit in, learn new customs, go along with the crowd, and find ways to belong. In many cases, this provides a wonderful opportunity to grow and to learn a new language and new traditions. However, it also presents real dangers when those traditions are steeped in ungodly practices, as was the case in Babylon. Daniel forged his identity as a young man amid many external pressures fighting to influence him.

It was not only the environment and culture that pressured Daniel. A strategic initiative mandated by the king was intended to shape him into a model leader according to Babylonian standards. Author O.S. Hawkins describes Nebuchadnezzar's plan "to corral the brightest young Jewish minds, immerse them in his own

Babylonian culture, reeducate them completely, and eventually send them back to Israel to rule on behalf of Babylon."[2] He explains, "Nebuchadnezzar wanted to change the boys' language, literature, and lifestyle, but his ultimate goal was to change their loyalties."[3] This was a plan of indoctrination, one backed by the richest, most powerful ruler in the world.

Daniel faced a critical challenge. In order to faithfully serve God in this period of transition, he could not emulate the culture he left behind in Judah in which God's warnings were rejected. Neither could he adopt the new culture of Babylon with its false gods, indulgent riches, and self-centered pursuits of power. Rather, Daniel needed to become a third culture kid, one whose identity was defined neither by his earthly culture of captivity nor the one calling to him from the past. God wanted a young leader whose identity was solidly grounded in his faith in the one true God; one whose hope relied on unchanging truth; one whose eyes saw beyond the noise, distraction, and ungodly attractions of the world in which he lived.

The challenge Daniel faced required incredible sacrifice on his part. In Babylon, he was stripped of his home, family, name, culture, and language. I doubt he found his favorite meal from Judah on the menu in Nebuchadnezzar's palace. The radically different manners and customs he had to learn likely left his head spinning, especially in the early days of exile. Furthermore, most evidence suggests the king made Daniel a eunuch. To avoid problems with palace officials and guards who worked near the king's harem, ancient kings castrated those assigned to these roles. For Daniel, this represented the loss of descendants and legacy, both of immense importance in Jewish culture. Daniel experienced plenty of opportunity to become angry, bitter, or frustrated with his circumstances. Why not embrace the new culture with its many comforts and opportunities? It would certainly have been easier to turn his back on God and adopt a victim mentality while clinging to his rights and entitlements as a Jew and believing that he deserved better. Would he, could he, lay it all down and become the leader God was calling him to be?

The Challenge for Today

I believe leaders today face a challenge much like Daniel's. The culture familiar to older generations is fading away, and with it, the values of the Modern era with roots in the Enlightenment and Industrial Revolution. Belief in absolute truth, faith in reason and science, and a sense of individual responsibility shaped America since its inception. As with every culture, there were strengths and weaknesses. While a strong moral code existed in much of American culture, many groups still experienced marginalization. Today, a new culture is emerging with radically different values and perspectives.

This state of transition provides the environment in which Millennials and Generation Z citizens have been raised and educated. As humans, we naturally absorb the perspectives of the culture around us. Not surprisingly, most young people today hold fast to postmodern values. Philosopher and theologian Frances Schaeffer explains, "Most people catch their presuppositions from their family and surrounding society the way a child catches measles."[4] Young people today are "catching" the values of an emerging culture that is very different from the one that existed just a few decades ago.

The idea of tolerance today embodies a significant underlying philosophy of the new cultural context. Hawkins explains, "Tolerance is the new buzzword and the new law of the land, and it has a different definition than it did just a few years ago. Tolerance used to mean that we recognized and respected other people's beliefs and value systems without agreeing with them or sharing them. Today, tolerance means that everyone's values, belief systems, and lifestyles should be accepted."[5]

Daniel and his friends faced pressure to accept the king's lavish lifestyle and to worship the gods dictated to them by the new culture. For leaders of today, there is pressure to affirm everyone in their self-determined truths regardless of whether those truths align with what God says is true. While modernism elevated the discovery of absolutes, postmodernism values tolerance above all else. Godly leaders face a mandate from culture to bow in tolerance to all beliefs and to allow all behaviors, even those they know will result in negative outcomes. Those who refuse to obey the cultural edict face marginalization and persecution. Like Daniel who was caught between Jewish and Babylonian culture, we face a shift from modernism to postmodernism, from traditional practices to more tolerant practices.

Babylon with all its enticements reflects the current pressures of our postmodern, globalized, technologically-connected world. While these influences may not be bad or wrong in and of themselves, they often become distractions and interruptions to what God is calling us to be or do. Whereas Daniel had fancy food and beautiful surroundings trying to lull him into a place of comfort and complacency, we are faced with bright screens, endless opportunities, and unprecedented access to information. If we are not careful, the opinions of others, along with the lure of our devices, or constant messaging from the surrounding culture, can actually distract us from our God-given purpose and godly identity.

Young leaders are often tempted to throw off everything of the past to fully embrace what is new, relevant, and exciting. It is easy to see what is not working and eagerly step into new models of leadership. In this pivotal moment, we would do well to pause and consider what elements of the past are godly? What elements of the present are biblical? How do we take the good of both while avoiding their dangers to live as third culture kids with our identity firmly rooted in God?

Developing a Godly Identity

As a third culture kid, Daniel developed an identity that blended aspects of his Jewish heritage with his new reality in Babylon. The filter for such an identity was faith in God and Daniel's commitment to obey his supreme laws. We see that Daniel retained the elements of his Jewish culture that honored God. We witness him honoring the dietary laws of God, praying three times a day, and reading the writings of the prophet Jeremiah. Still, he found it necessary to adapt to the context in which he found himself. He effectively learned the language and culture of Babylon while not becoming part of it. The ability to do so came from God as we see in Daniel 1. Amazingly, the king found the Hebrew children to be ten times wiser than all the magicians in the land.

Daniel's challenge is the challenge of leaders today. God allowed Judah to fall. He was working to purify and prepare his people for the promises and restoration he would be bringing. In that critical season of transition and uncertainty, he used leaders who were faithful to him above all else to orchestrate His purposes. As elements of our own culture fade, God desires to purify and prepare his people for the challenging days ahead. Once again, God is raising up a Daniel Generation of men and women willing to be faithful to their God despite what is going on around them. God is looking for those who can discern what is godly of the past and the present and use it to walk in an identity firmly grounded in an intimate relationship with Him. Will we accept the challenge?

Reflections and Applications

What leadership, ministry, and lifestyle practices have been a part of traditional leadership and church traditions? Are they cultural or biblical? Are they effective today?

What is it in our culture today that presents the greatest threat of distracting, undermining, or destroying godly leaders? How can we guard against this? What can mature leaders do to encourage and help young leaders within this context?

NOTES

1. *The Wizard of Oz*, directed by Victor Fleming (1939; Beverly Hills: Metro-Goldwyn-Mayer), Film.

2. O.S. Hawkins, *The Daniel Code: Living Out Truth in a Culture That is Losing Its Way* (Nashville: Thomas Nelson, 2016), 19.

3. O.S. Hawkins, *The Daniel Code*, 21.

4. Francis A. Schaeffer, *How Then Should We Live? The Rise and Decline of Western Thought and Culture* (Old Tappan: Fleming H. Revell Company, 1976), 20.

5. O.S. Hawkins, *The Daniel Code*, 72. 4

CHAPTER 5
LIFE IN BABYLON

I sometimes wonder whether all pleasures are not substitutes for joy.
—C.S. Lewis

If given the choice between eating broccoli or a donut, most preschoolers (and the rest of us!) will choose the sugary dessert over the colorful vegetable. A middle school student is more likely to choose video games over homework. As adults, we struggle to get to the gym regularly, spend money wisely, or manage our time effectively. There is a magnetic pull in our lives toward what feels good, indulges our senses, and makes us comfortable in the moment without regard for the future. If left unchecked, the human tendency is to pursue pleasure even if it controls and ruins us. Leadership in our Babylon requires a deep commitment to the pursuit of godly joy over temporary pleasure. So, let's look at some of the tendencies we need to be aware of as we live in an ungodly culture.

The Pursuit of Happiness

Our American culture reveres the freedom to seek what we want. One of the most often-quoted phrases of our Declaration of Independence emphasizes the right to pursue happiness: "We hold these truths to be self-evident, that all men are created equal, that they are endowed by their Creator with certain unalienable rights, that among these are life, liberty and the pursuit of happiness." The constant stream of immigrants to the United States of America demonstrates the broad appeal of this promise and hope. While none of us would negate the value of a country founded on such principles, as believers we must respond to God calling us to something higher and greater than what our culture promises, allows, or celebrates.

Ancient Babylon

As mentioned previously, Babylon boasted some of the greatest beauty, wealth, and indulgences in the world at the time. Daniel and his friends could have allowed their own happiness, pleasure, well-being, and reputation to drive their actions and decisions. The pressures around them were constant. Yet, we see multiple instances where they chose to deviate from the norm even at the risk of their own personal discomfort and loss. Daniel and his friends chose to drink water and eat vegetables rather than consume the wine and rich foods of the king's table. They repeatedly resisted the pressure to yield to the Babylonian laws that violated their faith, and never promoted their own interests or sought power even while in the midst of a very politically competitive environment. As we will discuss later, they found focus and discipline that helped them stand strong.

The 21st Century

So, what does the pursuit of happiness look like in our lives today? In 1985, 25 years before the introduction of the iPad, NYU professor Neil Postman wrote an insightful little book titled *Amusing Ourselves to Death*. In it, he discusses the power of technology to create a culture of "uninformed pleasure seekers." He explains how media slowly infiltrated our culture resulting in the promotion of entertainment as the acceptable standard of truth. Postman discusses writer Aldous Huxley's vision as described in *Brave New World*. The book was published in 1932 and set in London in the year 2540. Huxley understood that no "Big Brother is required to deprive people . . . people will come to love their oppression, to adore the technologies that undo their capacities to think."[1] In *Brave New World*, Huxley depicts the reality of people controlled by their desire for pleasure rather than by tyranny or pain. A century ago, the author feared that what we love and our need for pleasure would eventually ruin us. Let's take time to explore the role of technology today in our pursuit of pleasure and happiness.

Most studies show that the average teenager spends between 8-12 hours a day on their electronic devices. Many kids fear their parents are addicted to technology. They may even feel they compete with technology for their parent's attention.[2] It is true that technology presents the real risks of distraction, negative influences, and the pressures of our own culture. Notice that Daniel did not remove himself from places of cultural pressure, but he did find strategies to live as a godly leader in an ungodly culture. We must do the same. We will explore several of Daniel's strategies in the following chapters. Let's begin by considering some of the potential distractions to be aware of in our own Babylon.

Addiction and Influence

Technology presents several real dangers for us as godly leaders today. First is its highly addictive nature. Nicholas Kardaras, in his book *Glow Kids*, explains what he calls the "dopamine tickle." "Dopamine is the feel-good neurotransmitter that's the most critical element in the addiction process. When a person performs an action that satisfies a need or fulfills a desire, dopamine is released . . . into a cluster of nerve cells that are associated with pleasure and reward, also known as the brain's pleasure center."[3] This triggers a signal to repeat the activity again and again.

Today's technology consistently provides a dopamine tickle. Simon Sinek discusses its addictive impact. "The youth of today want to do good...the problem is... they're all addicted to dopamine. We pretty much raised an entire generation enslaved by the ding, buzz, beep, or flash of their phone."[4] Text messaging and social media notifications give us the same dopamine fix as gambling, drugs, and alcohol. In some cases, we can't wait even a few minutes to look at our phone. Playing video games, posting to social media, or watching YouTube videos can produce addictions like any other, especially if we fail to manage our actions and time.

The power of technology is its pervading influence in our lives. It guides our behaviors and perspectives by getting us to click on ads, buy things online, or read the articles fed to us. Technology makes it possible for companies to track our every click. Even worse, it enables the constant barrage of personalized ads, products, and information to invade our devices even when they are tucked away in our pockets or placed under our pillow. Daniel was subjected to a powerful program of retraining designed to influence his loyalties and attention. He completed the training, but managed to control its power to influence him. We must do the same with technology. While technology provides us with valuable tools, it also possesses the power to manipulate our time, attention, and loyalties. If we fail to manage its influence in our lives, we run the risk of responding to the powerful dings, beeps, and flashes of our devices rather than God's voice.

Pornography

We are subjected to an unprecedented volume of images, ideas, information, and people through electronic devices. Nearly three-quarters of all young adults (71 percent) and half of all teens (50 percent) encounter what they consider to be porn at least once a month whether they intentionally seek it or not.[5] Barna Research reported that "when asked to rank a series of 'bad things' a person could do—things such as stealing, lying, having an affair, even overeating—teens and young adults placed all porn-related actions at the very bottom of the list. In fact, teens and young adults said 'Not Recycling' is more immoral than viewing pornographic images."[6] The same report explained that young people placed "thinking negatively about someone with a different point of view" as a much worse offense than viewing pornography. This illustrates the distorted value our culture has placed on tolerance.

Barna Research describes the new moral code emerging in our culture as a "morality of self-fulfillment."[7] This code resonates well in a culture that pursues its own happiness. If one's actions do not hurt others directly, they are not considered bad. For example, many perceive viewing pornography as simply an individual choice. The far-reaching societal effects in the making and viewing of pornography include relational and sexual dysfunction,[8] abuse, and sex trafficking.[9] Nonetheless, for many people, watching porn is a personal matter. Because we live in an environment where porn is more acceptable and available than ever before, godly leaders face greater pressure to accept and engage in ungodly behaviors and views regarding sex and sexuality. If our moral code is not based on God's truth, we will be unprepared to respond in a godly manner when we encounter powerful outside influences.

Social Media

Social media, texting, and other forms of digital communication are effective tools for connecting people quickly and constantly. There is no doubt these tools are capable of enhancing our ministry, leadership, and relationships in many ways. Nonetheless, much research has emerged in the past few years regarding their potential pitfalls.

The term "Facebook depression" gained popularity several years ago as experts noted and documented harmful trends surrounding social media use. *Time Magazine* editor and writer Susanna Schrobsdorff indicates the rise of depression and angst in our society precisely parallels the rise of social media.[10] Overuse, or misuse of social media, results in individuals feeling depressed or discontented with their own lives as they view the highlight reels of others' lives. Seeing people's picture-perfect vacations, relationships, and possessions makes us feel badly about our ordinary lives. Instead of fostering joy and contentment, social media often drives us to seek happiness in fleeting things.

Social media plays a significant role in our desire to self-promote. In turn, this greatly contributes to the increase of narcissism in our culture. Author and researcher Tim Elmore reports that many of us are looking for ways to improve our self-esteem. We find an outlet on social media.[11] Social media, if we allow it, can be a tool used to pursue happiness, to feel better about ourselves, and to get attention. We must guard against the dopamine effect of affirming likes or comments on our posts. Sadly, this often takes the place of joy that comes from an identity founded in an intimate relationship with God.

Because of our pervasive use of technology, managing it well becomes critical to living a godly life. What this looks like depends on our personalities, struggles, and circumstances. I find that a regular "technology sabbath" in which I turn off my phone and laptop for a day, or even just a few hours, is helpful. It allows me to focus on the people around me or spend time in quiet reflection. It also relieves me of the pressure to respond immediately to everything. Taking time off for a personal sabbatical means that I am going to miss a few messages. The mental, emotional, and spiritual health that results from a technology sabbath, however, far outweighs the potential loss of a business lead or even a temporary misunderstanding with a friend. By taking a break from social media, intentionally monitoring our use of it, or arranging accountability for how we manage it, we are able to gain perspective that allows us to engage with others in healthier ways. It also helps us refocus on what is truly important beyond the lure of immediate pleasure.

The Pursuit of Joy

Our culture may celebrate the pursuit of happiness, but there is little biblical support for such a focus in our lives. Jesus challenged his disciples, "Whoever wants to be my disciple must deny themselves and take up their cross and follow me. For whoever wants to save their life will lose it, but whoever loses their life for me will find it."[12] The apostle Paul also challenges us:

> Since you have been raised to new life with Christ, set your sights on the realities of heaven, where Christ sits in the place of honor at God's right hand. Think about the things of heaven, not the things of earth. For you died to this life, and your real life is hidden with Christ in God. And when Christ, who is your life, is revealed to the whole world, you will share in all his glory.[13]

Scripture makes it abundantly clear that our focus should no longer be on this world and its fleeting pleasures, but rather on the promise of heaven. Society desperately lacks such a rich source of ardent hope.

Proverbs 10:28 declares, "The prospect of the righteous is joy!" Ours is the promise of a joy that is not contingent on circumstances, social media "likes," or possessions. Author C.S. Lewis puts it this way: "I doubt whether anyone who has tasted it [joy] would ever, if both were in his power, exchange it for all the pleasures in the world . . . I sometimes wonder whether all pleasures are not substitutes for Joy."[14] Can you imagine Daniel's joy in the lion's den as an angel shut the lions' mouths, or the joy he experienced after receiving a revelation from God about a dream that saved the lives of many? While life and leadership in our Babylon requires surrender and sacrifice, they yield deep joy! Life in Daniel's Babylon, like today, presented opportunities for him to pursue his own happiness and pleasure. He chose instead to pursue God's joy amid the temptations and pleasures that surrounded him. Will we ask for the courage and strength to do the same?

Reflections and Applications

What are my perspectives on pleasure, happiness, and joy? How have these been influenced by the culture around me?

How do I manage technology in my life? Am I addicted to the "dopamine tickle?" What can I do to better control its influence on my life? Is God calling me to a technology sabbath? What will this look like in my life?

NOTES

1. Neil Postman, *Amusing Ourselves to Death* (New York: Penguin, 1985), vii-viii.

2. Rachel Moss, "Most Children Worry Their Parents Are Addicted To Their Phones And iPads, Survey Finds," *The Huffington Post UK*, posted July 22, 2014, http://www.huffingtonpost.co.uk/2014/07/22/children-worried-parents-addicted-mobile-phones_n_5609510.html.

3. Nicholas Kardaras, *Glow Kids: How Screen Addiction is Hijacking Our Kids—And How to Break the Trance* (New York: St. Martin's Press, 2016), 36-37.

4. Simon Sinek, "We've Raised a Generation on Dopamine," YouTube video, 6:15, September, 25, 2013.

5. "The Porn Phenomenon," *Barna Research*, posted February 2016, https://www.barna.com/the-porn-phenomenon/.

6. Roxanne Stone, "Porn 2.0 The Sexting Crisis," *Barna Research*, posted April 2016, https://www.barna.com/porn-2-0-the-sexting-crisis/.

7. "New Research Explores the Changing Shape of Temptation," *Barna Research*, posted 2012, https://www.barna.com/research/new-research-explores-the-changing-shape-of-temptation/.

8. Brenda Luscombe, "Porn and the Threat to Virility," *Time*, posted March 31, 2016, http://time.com/4277510/porn-and-the-threat-to-virility/.

9. "An Online Epidemic: The Inseparable Link Between Porn and Trafficking." Fight the New Drug, posted January 23, 2018, https://fightthenewdrug.org/the-internet-can-be-a-very-unsexy-place-we/.

10. Susanna Schrobsdorf, "The Kids Are Not Alright," *TIME* magazine (New York: Time Inc.) 44-51.

11. Tim Elmore, *Marching Off the Map: Inspire Students to Navigate a Brand New World* (Atlanta: Poet Gardener, 2017), 182.

12. Matthew 16:24-25

13. Colossians 3:1-4 NLT

14. C.S. Lewis, *Surprised by Joy: The Shape of My Early Life* (New York: HarperCollins, 1955), 19.

CHAPTER 6
GOD'S HEART FOR BABYLON

I knew that you are a merciful and compassionate God,
slow to get angry and filled with unfailing love.
—Jonah 4:2b NLT

At the start of every year, I ask God to give me a theme or a word to focus on for the next 12 months. My word for this year, "love," surprised me. It seemed too simple. I have attended church since I was a child, read my Bible regularly, and sought to follow God for many years. You would think I would get the concept of love by now!

Here's the thing. I really love those who love me. But Jesus reminded us that sinners are good at that too![1] He asks us to love those who do not love us. In Luke 6:27-28, he says, "But to you who are listening I say: Love your enemies, do good to those who hate you, bless those who curse you, pray for those who mistreat you." Unfortunately, society often prepares us to reject this idea.

Who is to Blame?

We live in a culture of blame. People avoid responsibility while seeking to identify someone or something to blame for anything that goes wrong in their lives or in the world around them. We see this trend in politics, businesses, churches, and even in families and communities. As a result, we tend to view ourselves as victims forced to suffer the consequences of actions and decisions beyond our control. This mentality puts us into a defensive mindset in which we focus on what is happening to us rather than on what we can do to change the situation. This perspective of blame and victimization is one of the most powerful weapons the enemy uses to paralyze a Daniel Generation and negate its influence for good.

Daniel had plenty of people and circumstances to blame for the challenges he faced. These included previous generations who worshipped false gods, the prophets who predicted the invasion of Babylon, and his neighbors who failed to repent. What about the rulers in Jerusalem filled with pride and hardness of heart, or Nebuchadnezzar's tendency to be a cruel and ruthless leader? Of course, he easily could have blamed God. Considering what he went through and the loss and oppression he experienced, many today would encourage him to demand his rights! His story, however, would have been much different if he had given in to that temptation.

Instead of blaming others, Daniel chose to surrender

his rights and entitlements and view his situation in the context of God's greater work. He sought to understand God's heart, not only for the people of Judah, but also for the citizens of Babylon and their king, Nebuchadnezzar. This understanding proved critical to Daniel's success when God called him to serve the very king responsible for the death and destruction of his home, family, and land. Daniel was astute enough to know that there was no place for blame. There could only be surrender, humility, love, and obedience to the Sovereign God.

Daniel's approach to Nebuchadnezzar and Babylon went against not only the norms of culture, but also against every natural human inclination. To humbly serve one's oppressors with respect and dignity may seem absurd, but those called to accomplish such a task must decide if they are willing to align their lives with God's agenda. Authors Henry T. Blackaby and Avery T. Willis explain that when God is about to take a "step to advance His mission, He comes to one or more of His servants. He invites them to join Him, bidding them to adjust their lives to Him so that He can accomplish every aspect of His mission through them."[2] There is no room for blame.

God's Heart for All People

Pastor Mark Batterson says, "We pray as if God's chief objective is our personal comfort. It's not. God's chief objective is his glory and sometimes his gain involves a little pain."[3] If we are to participate in God's purposes on earth, we must set aside our selfish pursuit of happiness, comfort, and a desire for vindication in order to see God glorified in all things. In Psalm 67 we read, "Yes, may all the nations praise you. Let the whole world sing for joy, because you govern the nations with justice and guide the people of the whole world."[4] Are we willing to sacrifice everything to see people give glory to God, even those who are wicked and unworthy? As pastor John Piper writes, "At the bottom of all our hope, when everything else has given way, we stand on this great reality: the everlasting, all-sufficient God is infinitely, unwaveringly, and eternally committed to the glory of his great and holy name. For the sake of his fame among the nations he will act…He will vindicate his people and his cause in all the earth."[5] God invites us to align our lives with the glorious mission of seeing his name praised and his love displayed even when it requires letting go of our own comfort and interests. One other Old Testament prophet experienced this.

Jonah and Nineveh

The book of Jonah recounts God's dealings with Nineveh, the capital city of Assyria and easily the most powerful empire of its day. Nineveh was a godless, wicked city, and yet God called Jonah to go there to warn them of impending judgment for persisting in their wickedness. As we know from the story of Jonah's stay in the belly of a fish, he disobeyed God in this assignment. You see, Jonah came from the Northern Kingdom of Israel. Because Assyria was a national enemy of Israel, the destruction of Nineveh would have resulted in greater security for Jonah's country and people. He did not want God to forgive Nineveh because it went against his political views and interests.

After Jonah's dramatic experience when he ran from God and spent time with a fish, he finally relented and went to Nineveh. As he feared, the people of Nineveh listened to his warning and repented. Bible teacher Derek Prince describes what happened, "There is no other instance in Old Testament history of such profound and universal repentance upon the part of a whole community. All normal activities came to a standstill. The king and the nobles proclaimed a fast, and they themselves set the example."[6]

Contrast Nineveh's contrite repentance with Israel's own response to the many prophets God sent to them. Despite warnings from Jonah, Isaiah, Amos, Hosea, and Micah, the people of Israel persisted in their ungodly ways. Finally, in 721 B.C., more than 100 years before Nebuchadnezzar's invasion of the Southern Kingdom of Judah, the kings of Assyria captured Samaria, the capital of Israel. The Northern Kingdom was held captive by the Assyrians.

Jonah struggled to put aside his own interests and desires to serve God's purposes. If we want to be effective as godly leaders, we must seek to follow God selflessly.

If we align our allegiances with anything other than his purposes, we will never be able to effectively serve God in tumultuous times.

Daniel and Nebuchadnezzar

God used Daniel and his friends repeatedly to display his glory in Babylon. In Daniel 2, King Nebuchadnezzar demanded that his wise men first discern, then interpret his dream upon penalty of death. When God gave Daniel the revelation, he shared it with the king. Rather than take credit for it and potentially gain honor and prestige for himself, Daniel acknowledged before an ungodly Nebuchadnezzar that "no wise man, enchanter, magician, or diviner can explain to the king the mystery he has asked about."[7] Without any fear of what this powerful ruler might say or do to him, Daniel boldly declared that the source of his revelation was the God in heaven who promised to reveal mysteries. When Daniel finished telling Nebuchadnezzar what God had shown him, the king fell prostrate before Daniel and declared, "Surely your god is the God of gods and the Lord of kings and a revealer of mysteries."[8] Daniel's obedience brought glory to God even before a wicked king.

The Image of Gold

In Daniel 3, Hananiah, Mishael, and Azariah found themselves in a predicament. The king summoned all the officials to a dedication ceremony for the image of gold he erected. Everyone present was commanded to bow down and worship the image when the music played. Anyone who refused would be thrown into a blazing furnace. The three young, godly leaders stood erect in the midst their prostrate colleagues as the music sounded. I can imagine the scene. The horn, flute, harp, and pipes began to play. The mass of political leaders scrambled to bow down and demonstrate their allegiance to the powerful king. Then a murmur began. Someone near the three friends realized they were still standing. Whispers spread throughout the crowd, and people sneaked a look to see if it was true. Who would have such boldness as to stand?

Several of Hananiah, Mishael, and Azariah's Babylonian colleagues eagerly ran to the king to denounce the young men. A furious king summoned Daniel's friends and reiterated the consequences for failing to obey his command to worship the golden image. The three friends answered the king, "O Nebuchadnezzar, we do not need to defend ourselves before you in this matter. If we are thrown into the blazing furnace, the God we serve is able to save us from it, and he will rescue us from your hand, O king. But even if he does not, we want you to know, O king, that we will not serve your gods or worship the image of gold you have set up."[9] With this response, their fate was sealed.

The king was so furious with the defiant young men that he ordered the furnace heated seven times hotter than usual. The three young men were thrown into a fire so hot that it instantly killed the soldiers who threw them in. Suddenly, the king leapt to his feet realizing that Hananiah, Mishael, and Azariah were alive and that they were walking around. Even more astonishing, there was now a fourth man in the fire with them. The king called for them to come out. Seeing they were unharmed, Nebuchadnezzar declared, "Praise be to the God of Shadrach, Meshach and Abednego [the Babylonian names for Hananiah, Mishael, and Azariah], who has sent his angel and rescued his servants!"[10] The king quickly made a new decree that anyone who spoke against their God in the future would be punished.

Daniel and Darius

Nebuchadnezzar was not the only ungodly king to praise the God of Daniel. In Daniel 6, Daniel's new boss, king Darius the Mede who overthrew the Babylonians, issued a decree. The official decree dictated that anyone who prayed to any god or man other than the king during a period of 30 days would be thrown into the lion's den. Daniel, though, returned to his house to maintain his discipline of praying to God three times a day. Jealous colleagues couldn't wait to tell the king of his disobedience. The king, who greatly respected Daniel, reluctantly imposed the punishment. When Daniel emerged alive the next morning, Darius, like Nebuchadnezzar before him, praised the God of Daniel declaring, "For he is the living God and he endures forever; his kingdom will not be destroyed, and his dominion will never end."[11]

So, Now What?

In the book of Daniel, four godly young leaders continued to serve several evil kings and two great empires over many decades. By surrendering their own rights, interests, and comforts, to embrace God's mission in their season of history, they aligned themselves with God's heart for Babylon. They understood that God's love and purposes extended even to those who seemed to be unlikely candidates. The young men determined to make God's glory and power known to even the most wicked of men. This is crucial for us to understand today as we seek to lead in an ungodly culture. As Jonah declared, our God is slow to anger, but quick to extend his unfailing love.

Thus far, we have considered the challenges Daniel faced as a leader during a period of great turmoil in Judah's history. We have briefly discussed the season of change we are currently experiencing in our culture. Life as a leader in an ungodly culture comes with challenges as well as opportunities. As we reflect on God's heart for our culture, it is time to look at the practices that make godly leadership possible regardless of the incredible pressures, distractions, and deceptions that threaten to discourage or destroy us. How can we remain faithful and fruitful in our unique season of leadership?

Reflections and Applications

How would I describe my understanding of God's heart for our world today? What biases or perspectives do I have that might hinder me in aligning my heart with his?

Would I be willing to sacrifice earthly causes and interests for the sake of God's larger purposes? I know what that meant for Jonah; what might it look like for me?

NOTES

1. Luke 6:32

2. Henry T. Blackaby and Avery T. Willis, Jr., "On Mission With God," *Perspectives on the World Christian Movement,* ed. Ralph D. Winter and Steven C. Hawthorne (Pasadena: William Carey Library, 2009), 75.

3. Mark Batterson, *The Circle Maker: Praying Circles Around Your Biggest Dreams and Greatest Fears* (Grand Rapids: Zondervan, 2011), 113.

4. Psalm 67:3-4 NLT

5. John Piper, "Let the Nations Be Glad," *Perspectives on the World Christian Movement,* ed. Ralph D. Winter and Steven C. Hawthorne (Pasadena: William Carey Library, 2009), 68.

6. Derek Prince, *Shaping History Through Prayer and Fasting* (New Kensington: Whitaker House, 2002), 117.

7. Daniel 2:27

8. Daniel 2:47

9. Daniel 3:16-18

10. Daniel 3:28

11. Daniel 6:26b

PART II

ESSENTIAL PRACTICES
FOR LEADING IN
BABYLON

CHAPTER 7
UNDERSTANDING THE TIMES

These are the numbers of the men armed for battle who came to
David at Hebron…from Issachar, men who understood
the times and knew what Israel should do.
—1 Chronicles 12:23, 32

In the past couple of decades, the world has changed. As college students, my friends and I still passed notes in class. Today, we can video conference with people around the world, post images for hundreds to view in an instant, and even message friends in class without the inconvenience of having to pass a piece of paper! From advances in technology to globalization and changing worldviews, seismic shifts have occurred in our culture. Ideas and values emerging from postmodernism replaced those rooted in modernism. The internet now drives communication as connections are made globally and instantaneously. The impact of these changes on our faith and the church is significant as we must consider our response to new cultural norms, changing values, and declining church attendance.

In this and the following several chapters, we will focus on key perspectives and practices that allowed Daniel and his friends to thrive as godly leaders in an ungodly culture. We will also consider the implications of these practices for our lives and leadership today. The first key perspective—how we define reality—relates to how we understand the world. A godly understanding of what is unfolding in our culture will allow us to respond with courage and hope, rather than with panic or anxiety, to the changes and challenges we encounter.

Church in Crisis?

There is much angst in Christianity today over the state of the church in America. Emerging reports recognize and appear to confirm the trend of decline in the church. Some studies show that more than 4,000 churches close their doors every year. New church plants total just over 1,000, and half of all churches in the U.S. fail to consistently add new numbers to their ranks.[1] As someone who researches and speaks on generational trends, I am often asked about the state of Millennials and the church. Statistically, churches are failing to connect with young adults. This is backed up by the fact that as the Millennial generation entered adulthood, its members had much lower levels of religious affiliation, including fewer connections to Christian churches, than older generations. Of all Millennials, roughly 35 percent are religiously unaffiliated. Fewer than six in ten Millennials identify with any branch of Christianity compared with roughly seven in ten among older generations.[2]

What is Reality?

While we should not ignore statistics, we must be careful to understand our times beyond the research and reports (I say this as someone who appreciates research!). Author and teacher Francis Frangipane challenges our understanding of reality by arguing that "reality is not just objective: there is also a subjective or personal side to reality that is rooted in our feelings, attitudes and beliefs."[3] Faith in God extends our understanding of reality beyond what is seen, heard or reported. Faith is "being sure of what we hope for and certain of what we do not see."[4] Faith firmly grounds our understanding of reality in what God says rather than in our earthly experience.

Let's apply an earthly perspective to Daniel's life for a moment. If confined only to objective facts and what he could see at the time, Daniel's reality would have consisted of loss, captivity, oppression, and hopelessness. However, he understood a higher reality, one embraced by all the great heroes of the faith throughout Scripture and history. If we are to live as Daniel did with resolve to serve God's purposes, we must set our hearts and minds on eternal realities and hopes as we tune into what God is doing to establish his Kingdom amid current trends and changes.

An onslaught of opinions about what is taking place in the world today comes from every direction: social media, news feeds, popular podcasts, blogs, radio, and television. It is easy to allow these loud and constant voices to define our perceptions and understanding. While listening to a variety of perspectives has immense value, we must remain committed to defending what we allow to define reality for our lives. This is quickly becoming one of the fiercest battlegrounds on which we must fight as godly leaders who live and work in an ungodly culture.

Frangipane explains, "the essence of spiritual warfare is in who shall define reality: The Word of God or the illusions of this present age."[5] In the next chapter, we will discuss the necessity of studying Scripture in order to fully grasp God's reality. For now, let's consider what defines reality in our lives. What voices do we allow to influence us? Do they reflect the truth of Scripture and the purposes of God? We must accept, as Daniel and his friends did, that God does not measure success in the same way people do. Just as God's purposes prevailed in the midst of the destruction of the temple in Jerusalem, they will endure even in what seems like the decline of the American church. Like the heroes of faith in every generation, we serve a God whose purposes succeed even in times of difficulty or chaos. When an understanding of God's intent defines our reality, we can face change and complexity with confidence and peace.

Seeking Godly Reality

In 1 Chronicles, we read of a tumultuous time in Israel's early history when King Saul chose to disobey God. Because of Saul's rebellion, God spoke to the prophet Samuel indicating that he would raise up another king. God directed Samuel to anoint David as king, but it would be many years before the young shepherd would take the throne. In the meantime, there was much turmoil, uncertainty, and division throughout the kingdom as Saul defiantly clung to power. In chapter 12, we finally see men gathering at Hebron to turn the kingdom over to David as the Lord had directed. Among these were 200 sons of Issachar, men noted for understanding the times and God's purposes for Israel. Despite the conflicting views and political pressures of their day, they identified the appointed time for God to establish David as king. They were not influenced by opinions emerging from Jerusalem or by those being propagated through the social networking systems of the day. Today, we desperately need godly leaders like the sons of Issachar who seek God's reality and are able to understand the times and what God's people must do.

Prophetic Voices

In the following chapters, we will consider what it takes to grow as leaders who recognize what God is doing in our season of history. This includes knowing the Word of God, choosing godly companions, and practicing discipline and perseverance in prayer. Another critical tool for tuning into godly reality is referenced throughout Scripture, yet it is one that is often overlooked or marginalized in the church today. It is the gift of prophesy.

When we reflect on the five ministry gifts discussed in Ephesians 4:11-12, we find that some receive more recognition than others in many churches today. Most of us are familiar with the roles of pastor, teacher, and evangelist. However, the roles of apostle, and especially prophet, are often misunderstood or altogether disregarded. So, what is the role of prophesy and why do we desperately need it to understand how God is working?

Author and teacher Carolyn Tennant explains that the church in America is wondering how to respond to what feels like a crisis of existence. She challenges, "if the church chooses to answer this question merely through human reasoning, it will most assuredly fail in its paltry attempts. Our only recourse is to let God show us what we should do next."[6] While God uses a variety of methods to reveal his will to us, the role of the prophet in this work has always been critical.

In Amos 3:7 we read, "Surely the Sovereign Lord does nothing without first revealing his plans to his servants the prophets." We have already discussed several prophets including Daniel, Jonah, and Samuel. They encouraged others, whether it was their three Hebrew friends, an ungodly empire, or a rebellious king, by speaking of what the Lord was doing. Throughout the New Testament there are additional references to the role and importance of prophecy.

In 1 Thessalonians 5:19-21, for example, Paul writes, "Do not quench the Spirit. Do not treat prophecies with contempt but test them all; hold on to what is good." It is important to understand that prophecy is not a human interpretation or opinion. Rather, as 1 Peter 1:20-21 explains, true prophecy comes from God. It is for this reason that 1 Corinthians 14:1 challenges us to "follow the way of love and eagerly desire gifts of the Spirit, especially prophecy."

Prophetic voices serve God's people by providing critical insight and direction and by expanding our perspectives to see the reality of what God is doing in our times. We must study and understand prophesy so that we can be equipped to seek and recognize it. Prophetic insight must inform our understanding of the world today because it breathes clarity and purpose into the challenging assignments we face as godly leaders serving in an ungodly context.

As we consider the reality upon which our understanding of the times is based, we must rigorously evaluate the influences that inform our perspectives. Tennant explains, "When we pay attention to God instead of hearkening to others and to societal trends, He may well set us to doing things differently. We might be required to stand up against a popular notion of our times. We could be asked to do something unusual. When we have the courage to listen to God and follow His directions, the results can be astonishing."[7] Our approaches may prove to be unconventional as we follow God, but we can expect to see him move in powerful ways as we pursue his purposes. Frangipane reminds us, "We must see that our prayers, attitudes, and agreement with God are an integral part of establishing the reality of the kingdom of God on earth!"[8] This is the exciting role of a Daniel Generation!

Reflections and Applications

What defines reality in my life? How do I understand reality in the world today?

What voices do I allow to influence my understanding of the times in which we live? Do they reflect the truth of Scripture and the purposes of God? What voices do I need to listen to less and which ones do I need to listen to more? How can I do this?

NOTES

1. Richard J. Krejcir, "Statistics and Reasons for Church Decline," *Francis A. Schaeffer Institute of Church Leadership Development*, accessed November 2017, http://www.churchleadership.org/apps/articles/default. asp?articleid=42346&columnid=4545.

2. "America's Changing Religious Landscape," *Pew Research Center,* posted May 2015, http://www.pewforum. org/2015/05/12/americas-changing-religious-landscape/

3. Francis Frangipane, *The Three Battlegrounds: An In-Depth View of the Three Arenas of Spiritual Warfare* (Cedar Rapids: Arrow Publications, 2006), 107-108.

4. Hebrews 11:1

5. Francis Frangipane, *The Three Battlegrounds,* 107.

6. Carolyn Tennant, *Catch the Wind of the Spirit: How the Five Ministry Gifts Can Transform Your Church* (Springfield: Vital Resources, 2016), 121.

7. Carolyn Tennant, *Catch the Wind of the Spirit,* 133.

8. Francis Frangipane, *The Three Battlegrounds,* 111.

CHAPTER 8
KNOWING THE LAW OF GOD

Blessed is the one…whose delight is in the law of the Lord,
and who meditates on his law day and night.

—Psalm 1:1-2

"I have only read two books of the Bible," confessed one student at a Christian university. In order to prepare for church ministry, he was taking numerous courses in theology and biblical studies, but seldom read the Bible. While likely an exception among ministry students, his failure to personally study and know Scripture represents a growing trend of biblical illiteracy. As we engage an ungodly culture with a godly reality, we must not rely on what we think the Bible says or what someone else tells us it says. We must take the time to read, study, and meditate on God's Word ourselves. Only then can biblical truth guide our understanding and decisions.

Making Decisions

In examining the essential perspectives and practices of an influential Daniel Generation, let's consider how Daniel and his friends made decisions. Our culture used to rely on logic to make good decisions. Now, however, most people make decisions based on their emotions, experiences, and desires. If Daniel's friends had relied on logic or feelings, it is unlikely they would have had the courage to remain standing when the king commanded them to bow before a golden statue. In Daniel 4, we find the young prophet perplexed and terrified about the interpretation of the king's dream. Acting out of pure logic or emotion, he would likely have modified the interpretation that he shared with the powerful and unpredictable ruler by making it more palatable. Instead, he spoke the truth. So, if Daniel didn't use logic or respond out of emotion, how did he and his friends make decisions?

During their early days in Babylon, the four young leaders encountered many changes and challenges. They dedicated themselves to learning a new language and culture as they adapted to life in Nebuchadnezzar's palace, and even though they accepted some of the new requirements and expectations, they refused to adjust to others. On occasion, they graciously defied the dictates of their new environment and its rulers. Why the seeming inconsistency in their willingness to adapt? Let's look closer. In Daniel 1, we observe the first instance of their rejection of Babylonian standards. Instead of eating the rich foods served on the king's table, Daniel and his friends request only vegetables and water. Why would they go through the stress and work of learning a new language, but choose not to enjoy the benefits of a delicious feast from the king's table? This decision, like every other decision we see the four young leaders make, is explained by their unwavering commitment to the law of their God. Scripture had clear dietary rules for the Jews to follow, and Daniel and his friends were determined to obey God's law above all else. They based their decisions and actions on what God said, not logic, emotion, or cultural pressure.

Daniel also studied and relied on Scripture to inform his perspectives and his leadership. In Daniel 9:2-3 the prophet writes, "I, Daniel, understood from the Scriptures, according to the word of the Lord given to Jeremiah the prophet, that the desolation of Jerusalem would last seventy years. So, I turned to the Lord God and pleaded with him in prayer and petition, in fasting, and in sackcloth and ashes." Daniel based his understanding of current events and God's purpose for his people on Scripture. He accepted exile because he understood God's intent and timing. Daniel's decisions, actions, and perspectives were not arbitrary. They were not based on changing opinions, circumstances, or the behavior of those around him. Rather, Daniel remained steadfast in his decisions because he based them on the law and principles of God. To obey and align his life with God's Word, however, he first had to be well versed in it.

Biblical Illiteracy

Today, one of the great challenges facing a Daniel Generation is the fact that many of us don't know Scripture. Despite having greater access to the Bible than at any other time in history, with at least three Bibles in most American homes and access to digital research and study tools at our fingertips, we are reading the Bible less than ever before. A recent LifeWay Research study found that only 45 percent of those who regularly attend church actually read the Bible more than once a week. Even more astonishing is the fact that almost one in five churchgoers say they *never* read the Bible.[1] Barna Research reports, "Since 2009, Bible reading has become less widespread, especially among the youngest adults. Today, only one-third of all American adults report reading the Bible once a week or more. The percentage is highest among Elders (49%) and lowest among Millennials (24%)."[2] Despite this number, young adults who claim to be practicing Christians continue to say they have a high view of Scripture and refer to it as a primary source of moral truth.[3]

The American Culture and Faith Institute reports that the younger an adult is, the less likely he or she is to have a biblical worldview. Among adults who are 18 to 29 years old, just 4 percent were integrated disciples as compared to 7 percent among those in the 30- to 49-year age bracket and 15 percent among those 50 to 64 years old.[4] An integrated disciple is described as someone whose behaviors reflect their beliefs and who lives with integrity.

Godly leaders today are integrated disciples like Daniel who, regardless of living in a pagan culture, embraced a belief system grounded in the Word of God. They practice James 1:22, listening to the Word and doing what it says. The challenge for young leaders today is not only to live a godly lifestyle, but also to do so among ungodly peers in a culture that often opposes biblical values. David Kinnaman, president of the Barna Group, reports that the data regarding views of Scripture consistently trends toward Bible skepticism. "With each passing year, the percent of Americans who believe that the Bible is 'just another book written by men' increases. The perceptions that the Bible is harmful and that people who live by its principles are religious extremists are also on the rise."[5] Our culture is quickly moving toward not only ungodliness, but in many cases, antagonism toward God and his Word. In this context, God calls a remnant, the Daniels of this generation, to be bold, faithful, and godly! He is equipping us to make his glory known. In order for this to happen, however, we must study the Law of God, know what Scripture says, and live it faithfully.

Biblical Engagement

Significant factors in our society today hinder biblical engagement. They range from the skepticism mentioned above to the distractions of our many media screens and busy schedules that allow little time for reading and reflection. Yet, knowledge and understanding of God's Word are non-negotiable for those seeking to live godly lives today. We need biblical truth upon which to base our decisions, actions, and attitudes when faced with the pressures of an ungodly culture. So, how do we grow in our biblical understanding? What habits will help us in our engagement of Scripture and allow God, through his Word, to strengthen and equip us? Let's consider a few.

Reading

The Barna Research Group conducted a survey that provides some stark findings. Fewer than half of all adults can name the four Gospels. Many Christians cannot identify more than two or three of the disciples, and 60 percent of Americans can't name even five of the Ten Commandments.[6] The reality is that we cannot know what the Bible says if we do not read it. Yet, if we were honest, many of us would admit that we don't read God's Word consistently.

How do we combat biblical illiteracy in our own lives? Read the Bible! Yes, it is easier said than done, I know.

Here are a few simple, yet powerful strategies for godly leaders to embrace regardless of their age or experience:

- Establish consistency. If you find yourself in a place where you need to engage (or reengage) Scripture in a more meaningful way, start where you are rather than where you hope to be. Even if you only read the Bible five minutes a day, do it every day. Find a time that works best for you and stick to it. Many sources say it takes at least 21 days to form a new habit, so work on developing a healthy habit of Bible reading that works well in your current season of life.

- Increase your attention span. Most Americans today have an attention span of 6-8 seconds. Our minds are like a muscle and they should be strengthened gradually. If you decide to start strengthening your biceps, you don't begin by doing curls with a 20-pound weight. Instead, you will likely start with a 5- or 8-pound weight and build up to 20. The same is true of your attention span. The time you spend reading the Bible must be increased over time as you read for longer periods each day.

- Engage what you are reading. If you merely read for five minutes before going on with your life, it is likely you will forget what you just read. Take the time to highlight key phrases. Journal about questions or insights you notice while reading. Look up unfamiliar terms in a Bible dictionary.

Write a personal life application in the margin or as a separate note. Text or post a biblical insight to encourage others.

- Ask for understanding. When I was a child, my dad taught me to pray the following each time I sat down to read my Bible: "Lord, speak to me. Give me eyes to see, ears to hear, and a heart to understand what you are saying to me." That kind of simple prayer will position your mind and heart to receive from the Lord while reading his Word. As God speaks to you through Scripture, you will find the deep joy, peace, and purpose needed to thrive as a godly leader!

Meditation

The writer of Psalm 119:97 declares, "Oh, how I love your law! I meditate on it all day long." Meditating all day long requires more than a quick review of the verse of the day from a Bible app or a three-minute devotional. It involves allowing God's Word to permeate your heart and mind. Let's consider some practical strategies for meditating on Scripture in our daily lives:

- Identify key truths. Find a passage, phrase or concept from the Bible that really resonates with you. Perhaps it is one you feel God is speaking to you in your particular season of life. Repeat it out loud, pray it, share it with others, and focus on it while drifting off to sleep at night. Write a biblical truth on a sticky note and put it on your dashboard, computer monitor, or over the kitchen sink. I sometimes use a dry erase marker to write a verse directly on my bathroom mirror. Whiteboards in my girls' room and kitchen display specific Scriptures to meditate on or to use in prayer. Have fun developing and practicing other creative methods that will help you meditate on key truths and promises.

- Immerse yourself in truth. Use an audio version of the Bible to listen to God's Word while riding your bike, driving to work, or washing dishes. Listen to worship music or a good podcast of biblical teaching to keep your mind focused on the truth that enhances a godly understanding of reality.

- Journal your thoughts. Write down a Scripture, question, or idea gleaned from your reading or listening. Simply begin to write down whatever comes to mind as you think about it. Ask God to guide your thoughts as you write and to speak as you meditate on his truth.

Memorization

Memorization is another powerful way to focus on Scripture. The practice of memorizing has become a thing of the past. Why memorize phone numbers when we save contacts in our phones? Why memorize multiplication facts when we carry calculators in our pockets everywhere we go? Why memorize dates or details when we can simply Google the information in an instant? There are, however, some very good reasons for practicing the art of memorization.

Dallas Willard, professor of Philosophy at the University of Southern California, wrote, "Bible memorization is absolutely fundamental to spiritual formation. If I had to choose between all the disciplines of the spiritual life, I would choose Bible memorization, because it is a fundamental way of filling our minds with what it needs."[7] Pastor and author Chuck Swindoll agrees, "I know of no other single practice in the Christian life more rewarding, practically speaking, than memorizing Scripture. No other single exercise pays greater spiritual dividends!"[8] In a moment of frustration, temptation, or discouragement, we seldom take the time to search for a verse that will help us. If we have memorized it, however, the Holy Spirit will be able to bring it to mind and use it to inform and guide us in that moment. Memorization makes biblical truth readily available to us as we make decisions and interact with others. So, how do we recapture the art of memorization?

- Sing it. This is one of my favorite ways to memorize. Whether it is singing worship songs based on Scripture or putting our own melody to key verses, music helps us retain what we are learning. As I work with my children to memorize

Scripture, we will sometimes watch YouTube videos that set Bible passages to lively new music or tunes they already know.

- Visualize it. As you read the Bible, imagine a symbol or picture that represents each section or concept from the passage. If you are creative, draw or design images that illustrate the meaning of a verse as a way of helping you retain it. A friend of mine draws beautiful illustrations in the margins of her Bible that depict significant elements of what she is reading.

- Repeat and review. Obviously, the most important part of memorizing is repetition. Write the passage on a notecard and carry it with you. Instead of checking your phone for messages while waiting in line or stopped at a light, pull out your notecard and review the verse you are committing to memory. Car rides are one of our family's favorite times to review the memory verses we are learning.

Reading, meditating, and memorizing are just a few of the many ways you can engage and understand the Scripture verses that are foundational to your spiritual growth. Additional methods to help increase biblical literacy include taking a theology course, joining a Bible study, or discussing Scripture with a godly friend or mentor. When you know God's truth, it will guide your decisions, actions, and understanding. Biblical truth can set you free from lies and deceptions that hinder godly leadership. Knowledge of Scripture gives hope and perspective to successfully navigate an ungodly culture.

Reflections and Applications

How would you describe your biblical literacy right now? In what areas would you like to grow? Be specific.

List goals to improve your biblical literacy and grow in your understanding and application of God's Word.

NOTES

1. Bob Smietana, "Americans Are Fond of the Bible, Don't Actually Read It," *LifeWay Research,* posted April 25, 2017, http://lifewayresearch.com/2017/04/25/lifeway-research-americans-are-fond-of-the-bible-dont-actually-read-it/.

2. "The Bible in America: 6 Year Trends," *Barna Research Group*, posted June 2016, https://www.barna.com/research/the-bible-in-america-6-year-trends/.

3. "Millennials and the Bible: 3 Surprising Insights," *Barna Research Group*, posted October 21, 2014, https://www.barna.com/research/millennials-and-the-bible-3-surprising-insights/.

4. "Groundbreaking ACFI Survey Reveals How Many Adults Have a Biblical Worldview," *American Culture and Faith Institute*, accessed January 7, 2018, https://www.culturefaith.com/groundbreaking-survey-by-acfi-reveals-how-many-american-adults-have-a-biblical-worldview/.

5. "The Bible in America: 6 Year Trends," *Barna Research Group*.

6. Ed Stetzer, "Epidemic of Bible Illiteracy in Our Churches," *Christianity Today*, posted July 2015, http://www.christianitytoday.com/edstetzer/2015/july/epidemic-of-bible-illiteracy-in-our-churches.html.

7. Dallas Willard, "Spiritual Formation in Christ for the Whole Life and Whole Person," *Vocatio* 12, no. 2 (Spring, 2001): 7.

8. Chuck Swindoll, *Growing Strong in the Seasons of Life* (Grand Rapids: Zondervan, 1994), p. 61.

CHAPTER 9
PRACTICING DISCIPLINE

Jesus replied, "Cases like this require prayer."
—Mark 9:29 TLB

Several of my family members are marathon runners. After running my first 5K, I decided to adopt the less stressful and time-consuming role of cheerleader. I love it. I get to be at the event on the big day, stand in the crowd with cowbells, and cheer for the runners as they race by. It allows me to be part of the fun without the months of dedicated preparation that running such a race requires.

Marathon runners make a significant investment of time, energy, money, and pain for weeks and months before the day of the race. They often run four to five times a week and engage in numerous long runs of ten miles or more. These hours of running are not accompanied by cheering crowds. They might take place in the dim light of an early morning, in the heat of the day, or on a lonely path or quiet road. Practice runs require the runner to sacrifice something else: spending time with family, watching a movie, surfing the internet, or just sleeping! Completing a marathon, like most other important accomplishments in life, requires incredible commitment and discipline.

The Merriam-Webster dictionary defines discipline as "training that corrects, molds, or perfects the mental faculties or moral character." The Collins dictionary defines it as "the quality of being able to behave and work in a controlled way which involves obeying particular rules or standards." Few of us come by discipline naturally. Instead, we must diligently cultivate it. This usually requires us to establish a clear idea of the standards we want to follow.

Most marathon runners have a race time goal, the amount of time in which they hope to complete the race. This helps them determine a pace goal, the time in which they hope to run each mile. Disciplined practice makes it possible for them to meet these goals. Leaders also need to set goals and decide what they allow to determine their moral character and the standards by which they will live. As we already discussed, Daniel and his friends based their lives on the standard of God's law and implemented disciplines in their lives that allowed them to follow this law even when things got tough.

Daniel's Discipline

Scripture provides numerous glimpses into the discipline evident in Daniel's life. In Daniel 1, we read of his decision to eat only the food allowed by God's law. Chapter 6 records a most memorable illustration of Daniel's spiritual discipline. Verse 10 details his actions following King Darius' signing of a decree that prohibited anyone from praying to any god other than him for 30 days: "Now when Daniel learned that the decree had been published, he went home to his upstairs room where the windows opened toward Jerusalem. Three times a day he got down on his knees and prayed, giving thanks to his God, just as he had done before." This last phrase in the New American Standard Bible reads, "as he had been doing previously." Daniel's enemies already knew that he practiced the spiritual discipline of prayer three times a day. All they had to do was convince King Darius to issue the decree making such prayer illegal.

In the final chapters of Daniel, we see evidence of other spiritual disciplines in the prophet's life. In Daniel 9, during the reign of King Darius, we find Daniel reading the writings of Jeremiah, interceding, and fasting. He confesses the sin of his people and prays to the Lord on their behalf. In Daniel 10, during the reign of King Cyrus, we again see Daniel seeking the Lord and fasting. In this case, the Scripture says he mourns and fasts for three weeks! The intensity and time he spent in seeking the Lord demonstrates incredible endurance built over many years of prayer and fasting.

The consistent discipline that Daniel demonstrates in obeying the Law of God and reading Scriptures, as well as praying and fasting, was critical to his success as a godly leader in Babylon. The regular practice of spiritual disciplines kept him grounded in God's purposes and power. They provided a defense against the influences and temptations of the society around him and the pressures of his job and cultural context. So, how can we engage in spiritual disciplines today that will allow us to stand firm in godly truth as Daniel did?

Spiritual Disciplines

The Gospel of Mark tells a story that illustrates the urgent necessity of developing spiritual disciplines. In chapter 9, Jesus, along with Peter, James, and John, go up to a high mountain. The three disciples watch in amazement as Jesus is gloriously transfigured and appears before them in dazzling white garments talking to Moses and Elijah.

When they go down from the mountain, they find the other disciples surrounded by a large crowd and teachers of the law arguing with them. It seems that a man had brought his son who was possessed by a spirit to the disciples to drive out the demon. Although they tried, they were unable to do so. Upon hearing the story, Jesus cast out the spirit. When his disciples ask him why they had not been successful in their own attempts, Jesus replies, "This kind can come out only by prayer."[1]

Sadly, we often find ourselves as ineffective as the disciples who tried in vain to rid the boy of his evil spirit. We encounter a need, but when we pray, we fail to see positive results. It is true that God sometimes allows challenging circumstances to persist for our growth or for purposes we don't always understand.[2] All too often, though, we fail because, like the disciples, we are unprepared. We only need to look at Jesus' example to understand what is required to be successful. Even the Son of God consistently spent hours practicing the disciplines of prayer and fasting.[3] For example, he begins his ministry with 40 days of fasting in order to be prepared spiritually to meet the needs of the people. I wonder if many of the needs in our world today persist because godly men and women do not persevere in petition, fasting, and listening to God. Is it possible we are so busy raising awareness, reading articles, posting opinions, or fundraising for important issues that we fail to prepare ourselves spiritually to address them?

Prayer and Reflection

There are many resources available for those who wish to pursue the spiritual disciplines. I have included several in the Resource List. However, I want to briefly discuss a few important spiritual disciplines for godly leaders. In the previous chapter, we looked at one of the most important, knowing God's Word. Of course, intentional prayer must accompany this. I don't mean just talking at God, but rather finding time to be with God in stillness and reflection while listening to what he might speak to our hearts.

In his book, *The Shallows,* author Nicholas Carr describes how the internet is rewiring our brains and the way we process information. He explains, "We seem to have arrived at an important juncture in our intellectual and cultural history, a moment of transition between two modes of thinking . . . calm, focused, undistracted, the linear mind is being pushed aside by a new kind of mind that wants to take in and dole out information in short, disjointed, and often overlapping bursts—the faster, the better."[4] With the average attention span in America shrinking, it is clear that we do not spend much time in silence and reflection. Our brains are being hardwired to receive and deliver information in rapid snippets. We are developing the skill of "skimming" information to quickly extract what seems important and relevant. Of course, this skill is essential for sorting through the abundance of information we encounter daily. Nevertheless, we must make it a priority to consider practices and habits that will allow us to reflect and wait in stillness and silence for more than a few minutes at a time. There are many benefits for leaders who practice silent reflection, including decreased stress and an increase of mental function.[5] For those who seek to be godly leaders in today's culture, however, the most critical reason for finding quiet space in daily life is to talk with God.

Many years ago, I was a young leader under incredible stress. On one occasion, a panic attack sent me to the emergency room. I knew that something in my life needed to change. While reading the Gospels, I was struck by Jesus' practice of leaving the crowds behind, and even his disciples, and going into the desert or wilderness to be alone in silence and solitude with his heavenly Father.[6] After I read this, I implemented a regular practice that I call "desert days." While this time away has looked different in the changing seasons of my life, it has always required me to find a place of isolation—a cabin in the woods, a hotel room, a friend's home, a park, or a quiet room—where I can periodically retreat for a couple of hours or even a couple of days.

In most cases, I disconnect completely by leaving behind my phone, computer, and other devices. With only a journal, Bible, and a few books, I spend the time in prayer, reflection, reading, and writing. At first, I usually feel restless as I detox from the noise of life. Sometimes I even experience sadness as I wrestle with disappointments or frustrations that I had somehow managed to bury in my busyness. With patience, however, I am able to discover deeper understanding, fresh perspective, and peace of heart and mind as I reconnect with God through prayer, his Word, and by simply listening to the still, small voice of the Holy Spirit. This time away resets my perspective before I go back to my regular prayer routine and busy life. I have found that the practice of intentional and focused prayer and reflection is central to my spiritual, mental, and emotional well-being as a leader.

If Daniel, a leading official in a powerful empire,

found time and space to talk with God three times each day, we should be able to find a way to integrate prayer into our lives as well. Martin Luther, a key leader in the Protestant Reformation, is often quoted as having said, "I have so much to do that I shall spend the first three hours in prayer." The practice of setting time aside to engage in intimate conversation and fellowship with God is essential for any godly leader. The noise and distractions of life today require specific intentionality. We have a choice if we want to be effective leaders. Will we prioritize, like Daniel did, our communication with God before all else?

Fasting

Another powerful and impactful spiritual discipline in my own life has been that of fasting. I began fasting as a preteen because I saw the discipline practiced in my parents' lives and observed the positive impact it had on our family and their ministry. I wanted to embrace that in my own life. I have often found that fasting ignites my prayer life, advances ministry efforts, and increases my understanding of a situation. Even while writing this book, I found fasting vital for overcoming numerous obstacles. Fasting is so important that I try to fast on some level at least once a week.

You might be amazed to discover how often fasting is mentioned in the Bible. There are multiple instances of leaders who, in a moment of crisis, called all the people, even the children, to fast. In 2 Chronicles 20, for example, as enemy armies came against Judah, King Jehoshaphat proclaimed a fast throughout Judah. God's response? He enabled them to win the battle without even raising a weapon! In Ezra 8, the Jews who are returning from exile pray for protection on their dangerous journey through territory plagued by bandits and enemies. God safely leads them back to Jerusalem without a military escort or other physical defense. In Esther 4, the Jews are faced with destruction by a wicked leader. Esther's cousin, Mordecai, gathers all the people together to fast for the queen who agrees to plead their case before the king. God intervenes, and Esther finds favor with the king as her people are saved!

The Old Testament is not the only place in the Bible where we find examples of fasting. In the Gospels, Jesus not only discusses, but also models the discipline of fasting. In Mark 2:20, Jesus says, "But the time will come when the bridegroom will be taken from them, and on that day they will fast." In Matthew 6:16-18, Jesus gives instructions for "when you fast." Notice that he does not say, "if you fast." It is clear that Jesus expected his followers to fast.

Other powerful examples of fasting are found in the early church as evidenced in the New Testament. Some of the most impactful to me are those times when leaders come together in fasting and prayer. In Acts 13:1-3, we find the teachers and prophets ministering to the Lord by fasting and prayer. As a result, God gave them clear direction regarding his purposes for Paul and Barnabas. When they planted churches and appointed elders in the congregations, Paul and Barnabas did so with prayer and fasting.[7] Just like the godly leaders of that day, we, too, must make prayer and fasting a priority. There may be times when we call for others to join us in fasting for God to move in a particular place or situation. Fasting can and will increase the work of God in and through our lives!

Worship

Worship is a spiritual discipline that is sometimes overlooked. It is easy to become focused on what God can do for us rather than on what he calls us to do for him. Worship fixes our focus squarely on God, who he is, what he has done, his purposes and glory. Daniel 9 records the prophet's passionate worship of God as he prays for his people. In verse 4, he declares the majesty and faithfulness of God. "Lord, the great and awesome God, who keeps his covenant of love with those who love him and keep his commandments." It is in worship that we declare truths about God that bring him glory and build our faith. I often find that just a few moments spent in sincere worship can completely change my perspective and refocus my eyes on the greatness of the God I serve!

Like the marathon runner whose disciplined practice results in the ability to successfully cross the finish line, we must be willing to put in the hard work of disciplined preparation. If we are not willing to pray faithfully, listen in silence, worship, and serve with joyful diligence even when no one sees or notices, we cannot expect to see God move in and through us with love and power to meet the deep needs of our day as he shows himself mighty on our behalf!

Reflection Questions

What strategies do you find most effective for developing healthy habits in your own life? How have you applied these to spiritual disciplines?

What habits do you need to change? What spiritual disciplines would you like to further develop in your life right now? How could you do this?

NOTES

1. Mark 9:29
2. II Corinthians 12:6-10; Isaiah 55:9
3. Matthew 4; Mark 1:35
4. Nicholas Carr, *The Shallows: What the Internet is Doing to Our Brains,* (New York: Norton & Company, 2011), xxx.
5. Carolyn Gregoire, "Why Silence is so Good for Your Brain," The Huffington Post, posted March 5, 2016, https://www.huffingtonpost.com/entry/silence-brain-benefits_us_56d83967e4b0000de4037004.
6. Luke 5:16
7. Acts 14:21-28

CHAPTER 10
CHOOSING GODLY COMPANIONS

We expect more from technology and less from each other.
—Sherry Turkle

A friend recently bemoaned the fact that we seldom see each other. She expressed regret for not knowing what was happening in my life. Full schedules often make it difficult for us to find time to connect in person. As a result, we try to text each other, but those conversations often fall flat or remain superficial. When we do spend time face-to-face, my friend is easily distracted when someone walks past or when she hears the ding of her cell phone. As you might imagine, it is difficult for me to feel comfortable enough to share anything of substance under these circumstances. Even as I struggle to know how to better pursue this friendship, I realize that I am not alone. Most of us find it a challenge to develop the godly relationships that encourage and sustain us.

Daniel's Companions

Daniel encountered many challenges in Babylon. He was a minority, but even among his own people, there were those who often failed to understand the Lord's purposes. Nonetheless, he was not totally alone. A few faithful friends stood with Daniel through difficult times. These godly companions provided the support needed to navigate troubling circumstances in ungodly Babylon. Daniel relied on these young men in times of trial and counted on them for sincere prayer and encouragement.

In Daniel 2:5, we read that Nebuchadnezzar had a puzzling dream that he didn't understand. He called the astrologers and sorcerers together and said to them, "This is what I have firmly decided: If you do not tell me what my dream was and interpret it, I will have you cut into pieces and your houses turned into piles of rubble." It was a rather dramatic threat, but it shows us the kind of leader Daniel was called to serve. Because of their roles in the kingdom, Daniel and his friends were counted among the group destined for execution. What was a young leader to do in the face of such evil, opposition, and injustice?

Daniel's response to this trial provides a template for every godly leader. Daniel 2:17-18 explains that after hearing the king's proclamation, "Daniel returned to his house and explained the matter to his friends Hananiah, Mishael, and Azariah. He urged them to plead for mercy from the God of heaven concerning this mystery so that he and his friends would not be executed along with the rest of the wise men of Babylon." Like these young men, today's leaders need godly companions to stand beside them in times of crisis. As we read on, we see that God did, indeed, hear the cry of Daniel and his friends. He provided Daniel with the dream and its interpretation. God also gave him the courage to tell the king that it was God who revealed the mystery to him.

Daniel did not forget his God, nor did he forget his friends in times of prosperity and blessing. Instead of taking the credit for himself, he consistently gave God the glory. After recounting the dream and interpretation to King Nebuchadnezzar, Daniel received a promotion. The Scriptures tell us that when he petitioned the king on behalf of his friends, they also received promotions. Daniel showed himself to be a faithful and humble friend who was not afraid to admit that he had not navigated the crisis alone. When blessing came to him, he quickly sought the wellbeing of the godly companions in his life.

Daniel's companions didn't just support him through tough times. They shared his values and were faithful to pray with him for God's help and guidance in all their circumstances. The same dedication to God, faith in his power, and surrender to his purposes that we see in Daniel's life are demonstrated in the actions of Hananiah, Mishael, and Azariah. In Daniel 3, we read of the edict to bow before the king's statue of gold. They refused to do so despite the threat of death. Considering

Daniel's need for godly companions, how do we find and foster similar relationships?

Challenges to Godly Companionship

Let's look at some of the challenges to developing godly relationships. In the past 30 years, the way we connect and communicate with one another has changed dramatically. Many of these changes have been beneficial. For instance, my daughters can communicate regularly via video messaging with their grandparents who live in another state and country. My siblings, now scattered across many miles, communicate almost daily by using a messaging app. Thanks to technology, I can easily communicate with people around the world as I conduct my business from home. This allows me to be with my kids while doing something I enjoy. Some changes in communication and relationships for us as a society, however, have not been positive. In fact, some pose serious challenges to our ability to develop deep, meaningful friendships.

Decrease in Empathy

As mentioned earlier, estimates indicate that many teenagers and young adults use technology for 8-12 hours a day. While much of this is school or work related, a significant amount is for social or entertainment purposes. This has resulted in several troubling implications as it relates to our ability to establish and maintain healthy relationships. Empathy, for example, has decreased as technology has increased. One study reveals that college students are 40 percent less empathetic than they were 20 or 30 years ago prior to the advent of the internet.[1] Screens dull our ability to feel the pain and joy of others and to connect with them emotionally. This presents a threat to deep, committed relationships that are impossible to maintain without continuing empathetic interaction.

Narcissism

Another challenge to godly friendships is our perception of self. A growing trend of narcissism exists in our culture today. Author Tim Elmore reports that an overuse of personal social media platforms can foster a narcissistic culture. He cites that 95 percent of all young adults engage in taking "selfies." The average Millennial is currently on track to take 25,000 selfies over the course of their lifetime.[2] While there is nothing inherently bad about selfies, they do reflect a culture focused on how we look, our need to constantly document and share what we are doing, and our tendency to be overly concerned about how people perceive us. Researcher Jean Twenge reports that since the year 2000, narcissism has accelerated faster than in previous decades.[3] Traits of narcissism include bragging about personal achievements, finding opportunities to garner attention, and insisting on turning conversations to one's self. It is easy to see how social media can foster this type of mindset. It is impossible for godly relationships to thrive if we focus primarily on ourselves.

Reduced Attention Span and Commitment

Technology provides unprecedented access to people and information. As it relates to internet use, we must learn to be intentional without being obsessed by it. If we don't, we may find that we are increasingly impatient and unable to make commitments. After all, if we don't like a video we are watching, a song we are listening to, or someone we are communicating with, we can just change the video, the song, or perhaps even the friend. The plethora of options available at our fingertips makes it easy to give up and move on prematurely. This is evident in employment, within teams, our choice and use of entertainment, and yes, even interpersonal relationships. The godly companionship needed to weather the storms of leadership today requires a commitment that is often painful, sacrificial, forgiving, and unconditional. Unfortunately, our lifestyles today do not naturally help us reach this goal. Instead, we must intentionally position ourselves in a way that will help us continue to learn and grow as godly companions.

False Intimacy

In her book *Alone Together: Why We Expect More from Technology and Less from Each Other*, Sherry Turkle takes an in-depth look at how technology impacts relationships. She explains, "Technology proposes itself as the architect of our intimacies. These days, it suggests substitutions that put the real on the run."[4] True, godly intimacy in relationships often emerges from experiences like those of Daniel and his friends—praying, persevering, and enduring hardship together rather than through superficial connections and interactions. It can be tempting to substitute true intimacy for easy connections. So, how do we move beyond the superficial relationships so prevalent in our society today to those that will help sustain us in the days ahead?

Developing Emotional Intelligence

One significant key to healthy relationships is emotional intelligence (EQ). This consists of understanding our own emotions and those of others. Developing emotional intelligence and soft skills—those people skills that help you succeed in today's work environment—often requires more intentional effort than it did in the past. Due to the increasingly virtual nature of our interactions at home, school, and work, we experience significantly fewer face-to-face interactions than did previous generations. While Millennials and Generation Z individuals are especially adept at communicating online, valuable intimacy gets lost in virtual communications. Author Nicholas Kardaras cites a report by Quantified Impressions that indicates the average adult today makes eye contact between 30 and 60 percent of the time in conversation.[5] Emotional connection is built when eye contact is made during 60 to 70 percent of the conversation. When there is less eye contact, fewer connections are made. Virtual connections, while valuable, cannot replace the emotional connection and sense of wellbeing that occurs with eye contact, touch, and physical presence.

Consultants Travis Bradberry and Jean Greaves report, "Despite a growing focus on EQ a global deficit in understanding and managing emotions remains; only 36 percent of the people we tested are able to accurately identify their emotions as they happen. That means that two- thirds of us are typically controlled by our emotions."[6] To participate in healthy relationships, we must understand our emotions and manage them well. Failure to do so results in superficial or dysfunctional relationships and toxic leadership.

What is emotional intelligence, and how do we develop it as friends and leaders? Harvard Business Review reports,

> In his research at nearly 200 large, global companies, Daniel Goleman found that while the qualities traditionally associated with leadership—such as intelligence, toughness, determination, and

vision—are required for success, they are insufficient. Truly effective leaders are also distinguished by a high degree of emotional intelligence, which includes self-awareness, self-regulation, motivation, empathy, and social skill.[7]

Research shows that EQ is one of the most important indicators of success, even more so than IQ or experience. Bradberry and Greaves explain that it directly relates to how much we will make and how successful we will be in our work. "People with high EQs make more money— an average of $29,000 more per year than people with low EQs. We haven't yet been able to find a job in which performance and pay aren't tied closely to EQ."[8] The good news is that regardless of whether a person measures high or low for EQ, anyone can improve. Let's look at a few ways to increase our emotional intelligence.

Self-awareness is the first element of good emotional intelligence. Most of us probably know people who don't understand how they come across or fail to recognize the impact of their behaviors on others. Seeing others' weaknesses is usually easier than seeing our own. Being self-aware requires knowing ourselves well. This involves incredible honesty, authenticity, and humility. Without self-awareness, however, relationships usually stagnate. Many excellent resources are available for improving EQ. I will just highlight a few tips to consider for pursuing healthy self-awareness:

- Pay attention to your emotions. Watch how you respond to situations, and journal your emotions. Honestly acknowledge if you need help learning to manage them, and find that help.
- Seek honest feedback from trusted family, friends, and coworkers. Do not become defensive, angry, or discouraged with what you hear. Graciously thank them for what they share, and request their help in improving areas of weakness.
- Ask yourself why you respond the way you do and understand the values and views that motivate your emotions. If needed, find help to identify emotional triggers and learn how to respond more effectively.

Once we begin to focus on self-awareness, we are better able to manage detrimental emotions. Self-management is critical to relationships and leadership. Zig Ziglar once said, "You must manage yourself before you can lead someone else." Here are a few ways to work on managing powerful emotions:

- Give yourself time and space before responding to an emotionally disturbing text, post, or conversation, or making a big decision. Pause and reflect, seek wise advice, or sleep on it.
- Set aside time for reflection and problem solving. Our lives are so full of noise and distractions that it is easy to respond hastily and unwisely to people and situations.

- Find someone who is skilled in managing their emotions and responding to others. Ask them to mentor you. Be open to what they tell you.

As we work to understand and manage our own emotions, we must also increase our social or relational awareness and skills. Good friends and leaders pay attention to how others might be feeling so that they can respond appropriately. Social skills require constant intentionality throughout life as we engage different types of people in a variety of situations. Here are some good reminders regarding social skills:

- Engage fully with the person/people with whom you are interacting. Make eye contact and smile; watch body language and facial expressions; remove distractions.
- Practice the art of asking open-ended questions and actively listening.
- Build trust by showing you care by taking feedback well, by gracefully tackling difficult conversations, and by explaining your decisions and actions.

I encourage you to find resources to further develop your emotional intelligence no matter what level it is today. One great book to get started is *Emotional Intelligence 2.0* by Bradberry and Greaves. Leadership coaching with the Identity Profile Self Awareness Tool (IPSAT) or a similar assessment can also serve as a wonderful resource.[9] Most importantly, intentionally practice emotional intelligence in the relationships currently in your life.

Showing Ourselves Friendly

I have experienced several periods of intense loneliness in my life. In these seasons, my thoughts often go to Proverbs 18:24. As a child, I learned it from the New King James Version that reads, "A man who has friends must himself be friendly." That verse has stuck with me ever since. When aching for deep connection and camaraderie, I am forced to ask myself, "Have I been a good friend?" By doing this, I discover areas for improving and practicing healthy emotional intelligence, showing empathy, and investing in the most important relationships in my life. Periods of loneliness can be an opportunity to learn and grow. In my own life, these occasions have proven to be wonderful times of prayer and preparation for the friends God brings into my life in a later season.

We cannot expect to have close friends if we are not willing to continue to learn and grow as a friend. As we begin to relate to the culture around us, godly companions will play a significant role in keeping us focused on God's truth and faithful to his promises. These friendships are well worth the effort and sacrifice needed to develop and maintain them.

Reflections and Applications

Do I have godly companions my life right now, or have I settled for false intimacy? Do I allow godly individuals to challenge, encourage, and support me? What does this look like for me?

What kind of friend am I? Do I possess good emotional intelligence and empathy? Do I think of myself or others first? Give an example. How can I grow as a good friend?

NOTES

1. Pamela Paul, "From Students, Less Kindness for Strangers?" *New York Times*, posted June 25, 2010, http://www.nytimes.com/2010/06/27/fashion/27StudiedEmpathy.html.

2. Tim Elmore, *Marching off the Map* (Atlanta: Poet Gardener Publishing, 2017), 181.

3. Jean M. Twenge and W. Keith Campbell, *The Narcissism Epidemic: Living in the Age of Entitlement,* (New York: Free Press, 2009), 2.

4. Sherry Turkle, *Alone Together* (New York: Basic Books, 2011), p. 1.

5. Nicholas Kardaras, *Glow Kids: How Screen Addiction Is Hijacking Our Kids—And How To Break the Cycle* (New York: St. Martin's Press, 2016), 219.

6. Travis Bradberry and Jean Greaves, *Emotional Intelligence 2.0* (San Diego, TalentSmart, 2009), 13.

7. Daniel Goleman, "What Makes a Leader?" *Harvard Business Review* (January 2004), 1.

8. Travis Bradberry and Jean Greaves, *Emotional Intelligence 2.0*, 21-22.

9. See myipsat.com or leadingtomorrow.org/leadership-coaching.

CHAPTER 11
RELATING TO AN UNGODLY CULTURE

My prayer is not that you take them out of the world
but that you protect them from the evil one.
—John 17:15

For many decades, Christians in America enjoyed what some call the "Christian ghetto." A ghetto is a segregated group or area. While often used to reference an undesirable isolation, it can also be a place of comfort, familiarity, and safety. This positive definition reflects the ghetto of Christianity we constructed in the past. I believe that in the future we will see our culture strive to confine believers to a place of involuntary isolation and marginalization. Regardless, the Christian ghetto hinders our purpose as a Daniel Generation. Let me explain.

The Christian Ghetto of the Past

I grew up as a homeschooled missionary kid. Raised before the advent of the internet, my exposure to the greater outside world was limited. My studies and lessons were part of a Christian curriculum. Our home was always filled with Christian books. We listened to Christian music and most of my co-curricular activities involved church or other believers. I lived in a Christian ghetto, isolated in many ways from the world around me. Later, I attended a Christian university where we often remarked that we lived in a "Christian bubble" of chapel services, Bible studies, and theology classes. While these experiences helped to develop a solid foundation of faith in my life, remaining in the "ghetto" or "bubble" would never have allowed me to fully experience God's purpose in my life. Graduate school offered me an abrupt path out of the ghetto and served as a catalyst for God to work in and through me on a deeper level.

Today, many believers cling to their own Christian ghetto. They donate to and volunteer for Christian organizations, subscribe to Christian magazines or podcasts, listen to Christian music, and interact primarily with other believers through Bible studies, small groups, social media, and online communities. While these are valuable and essential experiences, if they consume our time and energy to the point that we never leave the ghetto and engage with people who do not know God, they can become detrimental to what God wants to do through us in the days ahead.

Beyond the Ghetto

After Christ's resurrection and ascension, the early church was launched from Jerusalem where Jesus had told his disciples to wait for the promised Holy Spirit. It was there that 3,000 people from diverse regions were converted in one day. Acts 2:42-47 gives us a beautiful account of the early church:

> They devoted themselves to the apostles' teaching and to fellowship, to the breaking of bread, and to prayer. Everyone was filled with awe at the many wonders and signs performed by the apostles. All the believers were together and had everything in common. They sold property and possessions to give to anyone who had need. Every day they continued to meet together in the temple courts. They broke bread in their homes and ate together with glad and sincere hearts, praising God and enjoying the favor of all the people. And the Lord added to their number daily those who were being saved.

Many of us long to experience the richness of fellowship and spiritual growth evident in the early days of the church. God's purposes for the believers even then encompassed more than a church club and the comfort of one another's familiar company. God's heart extended to the nations. The persecution of the early church scattered believers from Jerusalem, and wherever they went, they carried the message of Jesus with them. The remaining chapters of the book of Acts detail a powerful account of how the message of Jesus spread to Antioch, Samaria, Ethiopia, Rome, and beyond.

Daniel grew up in his own kind of ghetto. Judah was, in many ways, isolated from the countries around it. Life in Jerusalem near the temple of God offered an experience unlike any other in the world. Even though God encouraged some isolation from the other nations around Judah in order to protect them from following false gods and ungodly practices, the people disregarded God's commands and abandoned God's law to pursue the worship of idols. God's response was to allow the invasion of Jerusalem and the exile of her people. God, however, had a plan to make his glory known, even in a place like Babylon. This called for a Daniel Generation who understood what it meant to be in an ungodly culture, but not of it.

Not of the World

Jesus' prayer to the Father in John 17:13-18 reflects his understanding of what his followers would face in the days, years, and centuries after his return to heaven:

> I am coming to you now, but I say these things while I am still in the world, so that they may have the full measure of my joy within them. I have given them your word and the world has hated them, for they are not of the world any more than I am of the world. My prayer is not that you take them out of the world but that you protect them from the evil one. They are not of the world, even as I am not of it. Sanctify them by the truth; your word is truth. As you sent me into the world, I have sent them into the world.

Although this passage is full of powerful insights, I want to focus on just two.

First, Jesus does not ask for us to be removed from the world. Indeed, our presence in the world is part of his plan. In Matthew 5, Jesus clearly teaches that we are to be salt in this world. What does salt do? When shaken on food, it enhances the flavor. I occasionally complain that many of my close, godly friends live scattered across the globe leaving me feeling a bit lonely. My missionary

Dad reminds me that salt is not meant to remain in a pile unused. Instead, it should be shaken out to flavor the world.

Second, Jesus asks the Father to protect us from the evil one. He recognizes that as his followers, our role will not be easy. Real and powerful forces work to lull us into complacency, persecute us into apostasy, or tempt us into faithlessness. The appeal of the Christian ghettos we willingly embrace comes from our desire to separate ourselves from these evil influences and attacks. This is understandable, but no matter how we respond, we must not live in isolation from the culture in which God calls us to make his glory known.

Most of us know believers who abandon their faith saying that they want to make the gospel relevant in today's culture. They feel the need to participate in or condone certain unbiblical practices to reach their friends. Food, however, does not change the flavor of the salt; salt changes the flavor of the food. When culture begins to flavor and influence our lives, we are no longer salt. We must follow Daniel's example if we want to influence the culture, but not become part of it. To thrive in a godly lifestyle while engaging an ungodly culture requires that we have a strong faith, be disciplined, prayerfully engage the struggle, and maintain constant dependence on God. Relating to the world in a healthy way strengthens our faith because it forces us to know God's Word, to rely on the Holy Spirit, and to humbly seek his wisdom and favor as we interact with those who do not know him.

The Language of Babylon

When the Hebrew exiles arrived in Babylon, King Nebuchadnezzar told his chief of staff to train and teach the young men from Judah. Along with learning the language and customs of Babylon, Daniel and his friends likely studied the religious superstitions and sorcery common to the Chaldeans. The educational agenda for these young men was meant to result in a complete reconstruction of their values and loyalties. They had to resist the indoctrination of their new culture while gaining the understanding needed to serve an ungodly king while holding positions of great influence. Their intimate knowledge of the culture, its people, and provinces allowed them to serve in strategic leadership roles later on.

Today, believers who separate themselves completely from the influences of the world by sequestering themselves in the Christian ghetto seldom possess the ability to make a significant impact on the culture. This is because they have not taken the time to understand it. By contrast, even though Daniel and his friends did not imitate the culture around them, they were able to engage it in a way that brought them respect, even if not acceptance. They made an impact by literally standing out in the crowd! Our goal as believers today is not to be or do what the culture around us dictates, but rather to understand it so that we can effectively serve wherever God places us. The challenge of Daniel and his friends mirrors our challenge today. We must learn about the ungodly culture in which we live while avoiding its influence. I believe this is impossible without the help of the Holy Spirit. According to John 16, it is the Holy Spirit who leads and guides us as we navigate the challenges of living as godly leaders in a fallen world. As we embark on this mission, we must position ourselves to hear and obey his voice.

The Christian Ghetto of the Future

Today, a new Christian ghetto is emerging. It is not one of our choosing, but rather one being dictated by the culture around us. This ghetto isolates believers, limits their influence, and protects others from their views. It involves a process of marginalizing or discrediting the voice, traditions, and beliefs of anyone who says they believe in Jesus Christ. In his book *Is This the End?* David Jeremiah lists five stages of persecution: stereotyping, marginalizing, threatening, intimidating, and litigating.[1] We see the initial stages developing in our culture today as forces pressure us into establishing a philosophical and social Christian ghetto.

At a recent training event on intergenerational leadership, I facilitated a panel discussion of young leaders. One 16-year-old young man's insights were especially compelling. As the son of a pastor who had immigrated to America, he was passionate about his faith. He had grown up watching his father live out his Christian beliefs in tangible ways. The depth of this young man's commitment to ministry was evident to everyone as he shared his hope and desire for the church. He also confessed to the group that he never posted anything related to his faith on social media or acknowledged God with his school friends. To do so, he believed, would result in the loss of credibility and ostracization from his social circles. He is not alone. At another event, a pastor shared his story of attending a sporting event at a local school. While there, he encountered a high school student who regularly attended the church. The student, however, ignored the pastor when they met. Later, the young man apologized to the pastor explaining that he could not let fellow students know he attended church or he would be rejected.

Stereotyping of young believers occurs on many college campuses. A godly young woman I mentored shared with me her experiences while attending a state university. She explained that as she sat in class every day, she had to decide whether she would just sit and listen to the blatantly anti-God rhetoric coming from her professors, or choose to say something and be humiliated and derided by her professor and classmates. In our culture today, Christians are being stereotyped as narrowminded, homophobic, uneducated, ignorant, arrogant, or intolerant. Young believers often experience this to a greater degree than older generations. To label an entire group of people derogatorily is unquestionably stereotyping and the first stage of persecution.

In a culture set on silencing Christians, incomplete or biased accounts of both history and current events often paint the church as a villain in the real and painful injustices of our day. While the church is far from perfect and has often failed in its God-given task to promote justice, compassion, and peace, much of the story remains untold or is twisted in representations crafted by an ungodly culture. True Christians have always been intolerant of injustice. They have led key movements to bring freedom, justice, and peace in every stage of American and global history. Sadly, this story goes untold in a culture working overtime to remove the influence of faith from society. History reveals that successful movements toward freedom and peace seldom occur apart from the inspiration of faith. The history of Christianity as recast today represents an effort to discredit believers instead of accurately portraying the church and its important role in society. This marginalization is the second stage of persecution.

Other aspects of persecution already exist in our culture. Threats, intimidation, and litigation against Christians sometimes place their jobs, positions, and businesses in great jeopardy. It is a reality we need to acknowledge as we obediently engage our culture. The Christian ghetto of the past sought to avoid this persecution because it failed to recognize the blessing that comes with it. In Matthew 5:11, Jesus says, "Blessed are you when people insult you, persecute you and falsely say all kinds of evil against you because of me." If our journey of faith leads through persecution, we must never forget that blessing comes with it!

Daniel and his friends undeniably encountered persecution. Daniel's Babylonian colleagues had him thrown into a lion's den. Azariah, Hananiah, and Mishael were sent to the fiery furnace. Past and present stories of Christianity are filled with the faithful suffering of our brothers and sisters. In an article written for *Christianity Today*, Everett Ferguson insists that Christianity has never lost its martyr spirit.[2] He explains that persecution actually serves to bring people to Christ. In the early centuries of Christianity, people began to reject old gods as they saw the cruelties perpetrated in their names against believers in Christ. The testimony of the faithful forced them to consider the rewards of faith in God that were preferable to life itself. The same could be said of Daniel and his friends. Will it be said of our generation?

As we encounter stereotyping, marginalization, or other forms of persecution in our society today, we should take Peter's exhortation to heart: "Be careful to live properly among your unbelieving neighbors. Then even if they accuse you of doing wrong, they will see your honorable behavior, and they will give honor to God when he judges the world."[3] As Daniel and his friends discovered, humility, gentleness, and faithfulness in the face of persecution brings glory to God.

Reflections and Applications

Have you experienced the Christian ghetto of the past (isolation from culture)? What were some of its benefits? Dangers?

Have you experienced today's Christian ghetto (isolated by culture)? What forms of persecution have you experienced or witnessed? How have you responded? How do you think God will want you to respond in the future?

NOTES

1. David Jeremiah, *Is This the End? Signs of God's Providence in a Disturbing World* (Nashville: W Publishing Group, 2016).

2. Everett Ferguson, "Persecution in the Early Church: Did You Know?" *Christianity Today*, accessed December 28, 2017, http://www.christianitytoday.com/history/issues/issue-27/persecution-in-early-church-did-you-know.html.

3. I Peter 2:12 NLT

CHAPTER 12
SERVING THE KING

The heart of the leader is manifested through service to others.
—Artika Tyner

What comes to mind when you hear the word "humility?" I tend to imagine someone who is meek, reserved, or quiet. Humility is often confused with low confidence or poor self-esteem, or an unwillingness to fight for one's rights. Sometimes we mistake humility as weakness or subservience. Unfortunately, this powerful and essential leadership trait can be one of the most misunderstood and undeveloped qualities in our lives. Pastor and teacher Stuart Scott calls humility "the endangered virtue," but reminds us that it is actually the "root of every virtue."[1]

So, what is true humility? Humility begins with a profound revelation of our need for God. If we do not understand sin and repentance, we cannot practice true humility. The first step necessary for pursuing humility is to acknowledge our sin and God's grace. It requires us to live with an understanding of what God has done for us and is doing in us! Such revelation must come from the Spirit of truth because we cannot grasp it on our own. The truth the Holy Spirit reveals to us about our lives and God's goodness lays the foundation for pure humility to develop in our hearts.

The kind of biblical humility that is dependent on and obedient to God results in service to others. When we grasp the totality of our sin and brokenness without God, and the righteousness, purpose, and love we possess in him, we are positioned to walk in obedience to him. We can combat pride through our dependence on him when we are aware that it is only through him that are we righteous and worthy.[2] True humility remains confident and strong because it rests in the greatest of all powers. We walk in assurance because we serve in the love and strength of God. This is powerful humility— surrendered and confident. It is this humility that we see in the life of Daniel.

Daniel's Humility

Daniel did not suffer from a false sense of humility. He did not reject recognition or promotion. Neither did he deny the gifts and attributes God had given him. In fact, as Daniel 1:4 records, he placed himself in the category of "young men without any physical defect, handsome, showing aptitude for every kind of learning, well informed, quick to understand, and qualified to serve in the king's palace." He obviously did not suffer from low self-esteem.

Daniel, nonetheless, presents us with an incredible example of godly humility. Pastor and author Stuart Scott explains, "When someone is humble, they are focused on God and others, not self . . . they have no need to be recognized or approved. They have no need to elevate self, knowing that they have been forgiven and that God's love has been undeservedly and irrevocably set on them. Instead, a humble person's goal is to elevate God and encourage others."[3] Biblical humility allows us to serve others by putting their needs and interests above our own. Daniel's service to several ungodly kings models this kind of humility.

King Nebuchadnezzar was the first king Daniel served. This same man stripped him of everything—name, family, home, and legacy. The king proved ruthless in his dealings with enemies and friends alike. He was even willing to kill his own advisors. Yet, when summoned to explain the meaning of a dream, Daniel expressed sorrow at having to tell Nebuchadnezzar distressing news about the king's future. Daniel 4:19-20 reads, "Then Daniel (also called Belteshazzar) was greatly perplexed for a time, and his thoughts terrified him. So, the king said, 'Belteshazzar, do not let the dream or its meaning alarm you.' Belteshazzar answered, 'My lord, if only the dream applied to your enemies and its meaning to your adversaries!'" I might have been more inclined to answer, "Well, king, you are finally going to get what is coming to you!"

Daniel did not honor King Nebuchadnezzar because he deserved it. Rather, he served the evil ruler out of humility, placing God's glory and the interests of others above himself. Pastor Larry Osborne explains, "Biblical humility doesn't stop with serving those who don't deserve to be served. It goes one step further. It even serves God's enemies."[4] Such humility requires an understanding of God's redemptive power in our own lives. We cannot humbly serve other flawed individuals who need God's love and forgiveness without having experienced it ourselves.

Ultimate Authority

To have the kind of humility the Bible calls for requires an act of faith on our part. We must willingly surrender to the ultimate authority, the God who establishes all other rulers, even when we don't understand his purposes. Daniel's humble service to the king demonstrates his complete dependence on God. He instinctively understood the truth Paul wrote about in Romans 13:1: "Let everyone be subject to the governing authorities, for there is no authority except that which God has established. The authorities that exist have been established by God." Many leaders today are corrupt, evil, and unjust. This is nothing new. Paul, like Daniel, knew about corrupt leaders firsthand. Nero was the emperor when Paul wrote those words in Romans. He proved to be as evil and self-serving as Nebuchadnezzar. He inflicted incredibly barbaric persecution on the early church. It required great faith to believe that it was God himself who placed men like Nebuchadnezzar and Nero in positions of authority. Yet, God used both men while accomplishing his purposes at critical moments in history.

Pastor and author Larry Osborne says, "Daniel's humble respect was tied to his firm belief that God is in control of who is in control."[5] Biblical humility requires great faith because we must trust and engage God's plan, not our own, for our moment of history. Paul's encouragement in Titus 3:1-2 is one we should take to heart: "Remind the people to be subject to rulers and authorities, to be obedient, to be ready to do whatever is good, to slander no one, to be peaceable and considerate, and always to be gentle toward everyone." The response required of us in Scripture stands in stark contrast to the typical response we give to leaders in our culture today.

Biblical Humility Today

We live in a world that has become increasingly interconnected and interdependent. Power distance, hierarchies, and respect for authority are greatly diminished. Internationally syndicated columnist Moises Naim writes, "To put it simply, power no longer buys as much as it did in the past. In the twenty-first century, power is easier to get, harder to use—and easier to lose."[6] While technology provides amazing platforms for bringing awareness to current issues by responding to real needs and presenting diverse viewpoints, it can also make leadership extremely difficult. One picture, rumor of a scandal, or intentional misrepresentation of information by an opponent can paralyze the efforts of those in authority. The level of scrutiny imposed on leaders today is unprecedented making it easy to be critical, even hateful, toward those in positions of power. These attitudes, however, threaten to undermine our godly task of honoring and serving those in authority.

We live in a world where kids can post their opinions for all to read as freely as experienced experts. We spend as much time reading about one another's vacations as we do in analyzing critical international events. This tendency brings with it new dimensions of equality because it gives us all the same access to information and the ability to create content. There are few gatekeepers. In this environment, we often allow a picture, quote, or opinion to inform our perspective. All too often, we are distracted from the important by the attraction of the trivial. As we manage our time and develop perspectives regarding those in authority, we must be diligent to focus first and foremost on what God requires of us. Only then can we use our time and access to information wisely to help us serve more effectively. Above all, as we practice humility in honoring the authorities God places in our lives, communities, and government, we must remember

Paul's admonition "to slander no one, to be peaceable and considerate."[7] Humility before God requires us to deviate from the critical, destructive cultural and societal norms. It calls for firm commitment to a lifestyle of dependence on God and service to others, especially to those in positions of authority over us.

How does this look in situations where we are working with toxic leaders or individuals who are harming others? This is where we most urgently need to be engaged in the key practices we see in Daniel's life. As we study God's Word, consult with godly companions and mentors, and practice the disciplines of prayer and reflection to understand our own hearts and our context, we will find the wisdom needed in each specific instance. There are times where we might be called to disobey the king just as Daniel and his friends did when they refused to participate in ungodly practices. When we serve with humility, there will be times when God will use us to change the hearts of leaders. We see this in Daniel 6 when King Darius issued a decree commanding the people to honor the God of Daniel. In other situations, God may even call us to advocate before an evil king on behalf of those who are being treated unjustly. There is an example of this in Esther 7, when queen Esther risked her life to plead for the Jews who were about to be killed.

Larry Osborne summarizes our challenge rather poignantly: "If we want to significantly influence our modern-day Babylon, we'll have to change our tactics. Instead of avoiding or attacking the godless leaders of our day, we'll need to begin to engage them in the same way Daniel did, humbly serving whomever God chooses to temporarily place in positions of authority."[8] Daniel, of all people, had reason to disrespect his authority, yet he served loyally and humbly while earning the right to be heard and respected. James 4:6 reminds us, "God opposes the proud but shows favor to the humble." Daniel humbly served the kings God placed in his life, and God honored Daniel by showing him incredible favor.

Reflection Questions

What is your understanding of sin and repentance? How do you define humility? What does it look like in your life today? How would you like to grow in godly humility?

What is your response to godless leaders? How is God calling you to serve the "kings" in your life?

NOTES

1. Stuart Scott, *From Pride to Humility: A Biblical Perspective* (Bemidji: Focus Publishing, 2002), 17.

2. II Corinthians 5:20-21

3. Stuart Scott, *From Pride to Humility*, 19.

4. Larry Osborne, *Thriving in Babylon: Why Hope, Humility, and Wisdom Matter in a Godless Culture* (Colorado Springs: David Cook, 2015), 150.

5. Larry Osborne, *Thriving in Babylon*, 156.

6. Moises Naim, *The End of Power: From Boardrooms to Battlefields and Churches to States, Why Being in Charge Isn't What It Used To Be*, (New York: Basic Books, 2013).

7. Titus 3:2

8. Larry Osborne, *Thriving in Babylon*, 151.

CHAPTER 13
LIVING A TRUSTWORTHY LIFE

He was faithful, always responsible, and completely trustworthy.
—Daniel 6:4 NLT

I worked on the campus of a Christian university for eight years. One of my roles was that of overseeing our student leadership program. I loved experiencing life with young leaders preparing to serve in ministry, business, and education. Following spring break one year, I discovered that a student leader I had served with for three years had made some very poor and uncharacteristic decisions during a trip to visit friends. The nature of these decisions threatened her leadership position and graduation. I asked her to write out the reasons behind her choices and then come chat with me. She walked into my office, with tears streaming down her face, and exclaimed, "I don't know why I made those choices! I just went along with what everyone else around me was doing." Then she paused, and with great distress added, "I don't know why I make any of my choices!"

This revelation provided a profound insight for that

young leader. If we do not understand how and why we make decisions, it is impossible to live a trustworthy life. Our choices will continue to be random and unpredictable. Those working with us will find it hard to depend on us or know how we will respond in a given situation. Our lives will lack the integrity necessary for us to remain faithful to God and his purposes in the midst of intense worldly distractions and pressures.

A Trustworthy Life

In Daniel 6, we read about Daniel's jealous coworkers. God had blessed Daniel's life and given him incredible favor with the king. "Daniel, brimming with spirit and intelligence, so completely outclassed the other vice-regents and governors that the king decided to put him in charge of the whole kingdom."[1] Not everyone was happy about his quick assent to power and influence, so some of his colleagues decided to take him out. They searched for any flaw in his behavior or work they could use against him. However, Daniel served so well that his enemies could find nothing in his life to criticize or condemn. Daniel 6:4 tells us, "At this, the administrators and the satraps tried to find grounds for charges against Daniel in his conduct of government affairs, but they were unable to do so. They could find no corruption in him, because he was trustworthy and neither corrupt nor negligent." I am convinced that Daniel would have been able to stand up even under the intense scrutiny on leaders today.

Daniel rose to power because he remained faithful to God and God blessed him. He grounded his life in godly principles and served with humility and understanding. The king knew he could trust him to consistently do what was right and in the best interest of the kingdom. It is easy to understand why Nebuchadnezzar promoted him. Every company, organization, and ministry I work with today hopes to find this type of leader. A trustworthy leader must exemplify integrity. So, what is integrity?

Living with Integrity

Integrity is a great concept, but sometimes difficult to fully grasp. The Merriam Webster dictionary defines it as a "firm adherence to a code of especially moral or artistic values." In other words, it describes someone who faithfully follows a set moral code or principles. The Collins dictionary defines a person of integrity as one who is "honest and firm in their moral principles." As we know from our earlier discussion, the moral foundations of our culture are being shaken. In a culture that says morality is based on what feels right, there can be little integrity. I don't know about you, but my feelings are a bit unpredictable. What feels right at the moment can change based on whether I have had my coffee or someone looked at me wrong!

If we want to live a life of integrity, we simply must have a moral code and principles that are based on something other than our feelings or what people around us are saying or doing. Philosopher and theologian Francis Schaeffer explains that the flow of history and culture is rooted in the thoughts of people. "The inner life of the mind with its perspectives and worldview determines our actions and value systems."[2] Integrity and trustworthiness come from within us in the form of our thoughts, our beliefs, and our worldview. Faithfully following our beliefs results in trustworthiness and integrity. We must not be reactionary in our response to the world around us. Integrity requires us to do the hard work of first determining what we believe before we can be intentional in how we live out those beliefs.

Author and speaker Donald Miller wrote a blog entitled, "A Definition of Integrity That Will Change the Way You Live."[3] In that post, he encourages readers to develop a personal definition of integrity. He shares his own by listing things that reflect integrity in his life. Here is a sample of some of the items on his list.

Don has integrity when he:

- Stands in the authority God has given him
- Consistently contributes something positive to the world
- Allows God and trusted others to correct his path
- Follows through on agreed upon tasks
- Acknowledges God as his leader and Jesus as his friend

- Always keeps love at the core of his interactions with other people
- Does not default to a victim mindset, but takes responsibility for what can be done
- Is faithful to Betsy, his wife
- Is true to his creative calling[4]

Integrity can be hard to define and practice. Identifying our beliefs and putting them into practical terms will help us faithfully live according to a biblical moral code rather than simply responding to our emotions, people, or circumstances.

Integrity Under Pressure

If Daniel had written a personal definition of integrity for his life, I imagine it might have looked something like this.

Daniel has integrity when he:

- Worships the one, true God
- Serves the authorities God has placed in positions of power
- Puts the interests of others first
- Obeys the law of God
- Honors his friends
- Seeks to understand and follow God's purposes
- Prays faithfully

A life of integrity is seldom an easy one. In fact,

integrity often gets tested when life is most difficult. In Daniel 6, the prophet's enemies sought to use his most valued beliefs and disciplines against him. Daniel's coworkers realized, "We will never find any basis for charges against this man Daniel unless it has something to do with the law of his God."[5] Daniel was so faithful in his prayer life that his enemies knew he would not stop praying even if the king commanded it. He remained faithful to his personal definition of integrity to the point of death. He was willing to face a den of lions rather than deviate from his beliefs. These beliefs were the foundation of his trustworthiness and integrity.

What are we willing to die for? The answer to this question helps us determine what we believe is important and what we can live for in a trustworthy manner. For many of us, this is something we are still working out. We must prioritize this process in our lives. It will require prayer and soul searching as well as conversations with trusted friends or mentors. As we determine what we believe and begin to live by those beliefs, our actions become trustworthy and powerful!

Reflections and Applications

How do you make decisions? What determines your daily choices?

What does integrity look like in your life? Make a

practical list. Consider putting it somewhere visible where you can review it regularly.

NOTES

1. Daniel 6:3 MSG
2. Francis A. Schaeffer, *How Then Should We Live? The Rise and Decline of Western Thought and Culture* (Old Tappan: Fleming H. Revell Company, 1976), 20.
3. Donald Miller, "A Definition of Integrity That Will Change the Way You Live," accessed February 1, 2018, http://storylineblog.com/2013/06/24/a-working-tangible-definition-of-integrity/.
4. Donald Miller, "A Definition of Integrity."
5. Daniel 6:5

CHAPTER 14
SEEKING UNDERSTANDING

Life can only be understood backwards; but it must be lived forwards.
—Soren Kierkegaard

As a teenager, one of my favorite books of the Bible was Proverbs, written in large part by the wise King Solomon. First Kings 4:29-30 tells us, "God gave Solomon wisdom and very great insight, and a breadth of understanding as measureless as the sand on the seashore. Solomon's wisdom was greater than the wisdom of all the people of the East, and greater than all the wisdom of Egypt." Solomon likely wrote the words of Proverbs for his sons and other young people in Israel. I often have imagined myself sitting at Solomon's feet soaking up the great insights he sought to convey to the young leaders of his day.

The urgent theme of the Book of Proverbs greatly influenced my prayers and pursuits as a developing leader. Proverbs 4:5-7 sums up the passionate message Solomon sought to communicate: "Get wisdom, get understanding; do not forget my words or turn away from them. Do not forsake wisdom, and she will protect you; love her, and she will watch over you. The beginning of wisdom is this: Get wisdom. Though it cost you all you have, get understanding."

What is worth the price of all we have? Solomon claims that it is wisdom and understanding. He insists they are more valuable than gold or rubies. As a teenager, I began to pray consistently for wisdom. I sought it out. When I stepped into various leadership roles as a college student and young adult, the value of wisdom and understanding became evident to me. Even after several decades of serving in various leadership roles, I continue to treasure the pursuit of wisdom above all other leadership qualities. One of my regular prayers today is for God to give my own children his wisdom and understanding that they, too, will desire and pursue it with all their hearts.

The Search for Wisdom

The Merriam-Webster dictionary defines wisdom as the "ability to discern inner qualities and relationships, or good sense." According to the Collins dictionary, it "is the ability to use your experience and knowledge to make sensible decisions or judgments." It is evident why leaders need wisdom. In Proverbs 9:10, we discover the source of biblical wisdom: "The fear of the Lord is the beginning of wisdom, and knowledge of the Holy One is understanding." Fear in this case means to honor or revere above all else. Wisdom is gained when we love God so deeply and understand his holy character so profoundly that we fear disobeying or disregarding his commands and principles. Obedience and surrender to God propel us into wise action. So, how do we practically pursue godly wisdom?

Ask for Wisdom

The first thing we must do in our search for wisdom is ask for it. James 1:5 tells us, "If any of you lacks wisdom, you should ask God, who gives generously to all without finding fault, and it will be given to you." This may seem simple, but it is crucial. Matthew 7:7-8 reminds us, "Ask and it will be given to you; seek and you will find; knock and the door will be opened to you. For everyone who asks receives; the one who seeks finds." Solomon displays a passion and intensity as he seeks godly understanding. In Proverbs 2:3-5 he explains, "Indeed, if you call out for insight and cry aloud for understanding, and if you look for it as for silver and search for it as for hidden treasure, then you will understand the fear of the Lord." Sound judgment grounded in a healthy fear of God is vital to godly leaders serving in an ungodly culture. It is worth "crying aloud" for it!

Listen for Wisdom

I love the picture of wisdom that Solomon paints for us in Proverbs 1:20-23: "Out in the open wisdom calls aloud, she raises her voice in the public square; on top of the wall she cries out, at the city gate she makes her speech: 'How long will you who are simple love your simple ways? Repent at my rebuke! Then I will pour out my thoughts to you, I will make known to you my teachings.'" I can just imagine wisdom's frustration as she stands on the wall watching the simple and foolish disregard her teaching. That picture is motivating to me. It makes me want to live and lead in such a way that wisdom would smile down at me! I want to soak up the thoughts and teachings of godly wisdom! How do I do that?

God often answers my prayers for wisdom through the disciplines of prayer, silence, and reflection discussed earlier. I have made plenty of unwise decisions in moments of stress or busyness, or in response to the pressure and perspectives of others. The decisions that I pray over, reflect upon, and measure against Scriptures prove to be creative, productive, and life giving. Decisions made as I listen for wisdom set me free from guilt, worry, or fear. They allow me to proceed in confidence knowing they were made in prayerful thoughtfulness.

Seek Out Wisdom

Another way God answers my prayer for wisdom is through interactions with those who possess more knowledge or experience than I do. I find that diversity in relationships is invaluable in this regard. Those who are older than I am provide perspective, insights, and wisdom from their wealth of experience and years of service. Those who are younger than I am provide understanding of culture and perspective on challenges I no longer face. It is extremely beneficial for me to engage in conversation with those whose perspectives differ from my own. While I may not always agree with what they say, I gain a better understanding as I hear their point of view. One of my favorite ways of seeking understanding is to read about men and women of faith and influence throughout history. It is amazing how the voices of individuals who lived centuries ago reach out and provide insight into my life today.

Daniel's Understanding

In Daniel 9:2-3, we read of the prophet's pursuit of understanding. "In the first year of his [Darius'] reign, I, Daniel, understood from the Scriptures, according to the word of the Lord given to Jeremiah the prophet, that the desolation of Jerusalem would last seventy years. So, I turned to the Lord God and pleaded with him in prayer and petition, in fasting, and in sackcloth and ashes." Daniel was not simply a leader serving the king in Babylon. He was also a spiritual leader pursuing God's will for his people. In this passage, we find him seeking God's purpose for those living in exile.

Babylon fell to the Medes and Persians in 539 B.C. It was during that time that Darius became king. The first year of his reign would have been roughly 66 years after Daniel arrived in Babylon. In Daniel 9, he was probably around 80 years old. Yet, even in this mature season of life, he continued to seek understanding. He read the words of Jeremiah the prophet who had warned Judah to repent. The people's disregard for God's warnings spoken through Jeremiah resulted in the Babylonian exile. Decades later, we find Daniel reading the words of this man of God who by now had been dead for years.

A couple of things strike me from the passage in Daniel 9. The first is that we should never stop seeking understanding. If Daniel continued to learn at the age of 80, so must we. The second is that he never stopped leading. Even in this advanced stage of life, he prayed and believed for God's will to be accomplished in the lives of his people. Daniel 9-10 reveals his spiritual leadership continuing through his intercession for God's people.

I am also intrigued by the lasting impact of Jeremiah's godly life. I believe there are many experienced leaders among us who will play the role of Jeremiah in the lives of the next generation. Their faithful service to God in a season of upheaval and transition will leave a legacy of truth that the Daniels of the next generation will find encouraging and sorely needed in days to come.

In the next section of this book, we will look at some of the broader changes occurring in leadership today as we navigate a significant cultural shift. To lead effectively in this context, however, we need to put into practice the critical disciplines seen in Daniel's life. As we engage the culture around us, we must value godly companions, know and understand God's Word, practice godly disciplines, and become equipped to live trustworthy lives with godly wisdom. I believe God is positioning a remnant of godly leaders in this season who will experience his power and glory in miraculous ways! Are you ready to be his remnant?

Reflection Questions

How do you seek wisdom in your life? What practices or relationships has God used to give you godly insight and understanding?

How do you want to continue to grow in biblical wisdom and understanding? What can you do in a practical way to pursue this?

PART III

LEADERSHIP
PERSPECTIVES

CHAPTER 15
LEADERSHIP REDEFINED

Although we intuitively know the world has changed, most leaders reflect
a model and leader development process that are sorely out of date.
—General Stanley McChrystal

My earliest memories are of life on the family farm. As a little girl, I loved feeding the baby calves with huge bottles of milk and playing in the warm, sweet-smelling barn while Dad fed the cows. My siblings and I imagined grand adventures as we played in the corncrib and skipped rocks in the creek behind our house. Best of all, though, were tractor rides with Dad or Grandpa! It was thrilling to be up on that big machine watching it do its work in the fields.

Both of my grandpas were farmers. My dad was also a farmer until I was seven, when God called our family to missions. As a little girl, I was privileged to experience the rhythms of farm life. In the spring, we picked up rocks and prepared the fields for sowing. In the summer, we sprayed and fertilized the crops to kill bugs and weeds that threatened their growth. The days of fall were long and busy as we harvested crops, but we always left the ground to rest for the winter in preparation for spring planting. Each season had a purpose that called for different tasks and tools. If a plow were used in the summer, it would destroy the growing plants. If fertilizer were sprayed in the winter, there would be no seeds to benefit from it.

Changing seasons on the farm remind me of different eras in culture. Each has a purpose and requires different approaches and tools. When we talk about new leadership strategies, experienced leaders can sometimes feel discouraged. It is easy to assume that we need new methods because the old ones were thought to be wrong or ineffective. However, the opposite is often true. A new season with new needs may indicate that effective work occurred in past seasons. When a combine goes into the field to harvest a plentiful crop, it means the plow did its work well in the spring and the sprayer was effective in the summer. A good crop proves that the right tools and strategies were used in previous seasons. As we enter a new season in history, we can see the effectiveness of many previous leadership methods even as we consider what new models and methods of leadership will be most beneficial going forward.

Leading Amid Cultural Change

In previous chapters, we examined key practices for godly leaders living in an ungodly culture. In these last few chapters, we will consider necessary changes in leadership philosophies and methods for an emerging season.

Leadership in the Modern Era had deep roots in the Industrial Revolution with its focus on efficiency, productivity, and factory-style work environments. In this context, top-down, directive-style management seemed effective. Leaders were seen as the source of all knowledge and direction. An organization or team's success often relied on the charisma, competency, and skills of the leader. The role of leaders was paramount.

As we navigate the cultural earthquake occurring today, much is changing regarding what we need and expect from leaders. The amount of information available, the speed of communication, and the globalization of our society make it impossible for any one person to be the source of all the knowledge required for a specific context. General Stanley McChrystal explains, "The heroic 'hands-on' leader whose personal competence and force of will dominated battlefields and boardrooms for generations has been overwhelmed by accelerating speed, swelling complexity, and interdependence."[1] He adds, "Today's rapidly changing world...means that organizations everywhere are now facing dizzying challenges...these issues can be solved only by creating sustained organizational adaptability through the establishment of a team of teams."[2]

Amid dramatic change, adaptability must replace efficiency as a priority. As leaders, we cannot be the source of all knowledge. Rather, we must facilitate the bringing together of those who can provide a variety of perspectives and specializations. Today, leadership requires equipping, empowering, and delegating tasks to others so that together we can navigate the changing terrain. As McChrystal says, "The temptation to lead as a chess master, controlling each move of the organization, must give way to an approach as a gardener, enabling rather than directing."[3]

The metaphor of a leader as a gardener is an incredibly powerful one. A gardener does not grow the crops, but instead provides the resources and environment the plants need to grow. This requires the gardener to know the plants and what they need to thrive: the type of soil, level of sunlight, and amount of water. Rather than focusing primarily on the process or the product as in the past, leaders now must focus primarily on people by enabling them to complete the process or create the product. Empowered people and teams adapt more readily to ongoing changes by finding new ways to move forward when old processes become ineffective. This adaptability allows teams and organizations to survive and thrive even during times of great change. This style of leadership, however, requires a completely different approach than many leaders learned in the past. I have included some of my favorite materials on developing adaptable leadership and healthy team environments in the Resource List at the end of the book for those who would like to further study this topic.

Biblical Leadership Amid Change

Cultural shifts provide exciting opportunities to examine current methods and motives.

Leadership structures within the church today often reflect effective business models rather than those based on scriptural principles. For instance, associate, executive, and senior pastor positions look very much like their counterparts in corporate America. This is not necessarily bad. Culture will naturally influence the way we practice our faith. This is true around the world. Cultural shifts force us to revisit the biblical foundations that determine who we are, what we are meant to do, and why we are meant to do it. In other words, as culture changes, we must not look to cultural norms, but rather reestablish biblical norms. When we do, it is possible to experience powerful spiritual movements in seasons of cultural change. We see evidence of this in the Protestant Reformation that took place during the Renaissance. We also see this in the Great Awakenings that occurred during the Enlightenment and the Industrial Revolution. I believe we should also expect to see God move in powerful ways in our current season of change.

The early church revealed in the New Testament provides a compelling example of biblical leadership in seasons of change. Talk about cultural shifts! The message of Jesus' death and resurrection effectively upended centuries of Jewish tradition. The resulting growth provided a great deal of excitement, but it was not without challenges. The apostles definitely had their hands full with encouraging, correcting, and guiding young believers and leaders. Their guidance to the early church provides essential direction for us today.

In his letters to the churches in Corinth and Rome, Paul uses the metaphor of a body to explain how each believer has a unique and specific part to play in God's work.[4] No part is more important than the others, and all are needed for the body to function well. As leaders, we need to begin by knowing and understanding our gifts and the role we play in the Body of Christ. This goes far beyond having a particular title or position in an organization or church. We must develop, then grow in our gifts by faithfully using them as God directs. The first step is to understand how God has wired us. Mentors, leadership coaches, spiritual gifts tests, and practical experience can help us identify and understand our gifts.

Just as a gardener must provide the resources and environment for each plant to grow, godly leaders must equip and empower others to use their unique gifts effectively. The Resource List includes information on the IPSAT (Identity Profile Self Awareness Tool) small group model as an example of a tool that can be used for helping leaders accomplish this. Today's cultural context requires every believer to be equipped and empowered to do ministry. In the past, we expected people to come to church where those in vocational pastoral roles provided ministry. However, church attendance is no longer what it used to be. As a result, ministry must move more actively beyond the church walls. What is needed is an active priesthood of all believers—men and women who are anointed, equipped, and dedicated to serve God wherever they live and work. I can't help but be excited by this because it illustrates God's love and presence extending beyond the church walls to the world around us!

In the early church, God allowed persecution to force his followers away from their homes to take the message of Jesus to faraway places. In a similar fashion, today's crisis of empty pews presents an opportunity for the Body of Christ to transport the truth and power of God's love to our communities and workplaces. The season for charismatic, heroic ministry chess masters is past. In its place, we need new ministry gardeners. In other words, instead of leaders who simply move people around, we need those who will equip and encourage fellow believers to join them in the work of God's kingdom!

Prayer and Fasting

I earned a doctorate in leadership in 2012 and have taught leadership seminars and courses in faith-based contexts for many years. I am a firm believer in learning from others, adopting best practices, and having a vision and strategy. It strikes me, though, that it is tempting for us as leaders to put our faith in human processes and structures. Note the hiring and selection models practiced by leaders in the New Testament:

Now in the church at Antioch there were prophets and teachers: Barnabas, Simeon called Niger, Lucius of Cyrene, Manaen (who had been brought up with Herod the tetrarch) and Saul. While they were worshiping the Lord and fasting, the Holy Spirit said, "Set apart for me Barnabas and Saul for the work to which I have called them." So, after they had fasted and prayed, they placed their hands on them and sent them off."[5]

First, their roles were identified as prophets and teachers. In essence, their positions were defined by their ministry gifts! Next, they gathered together to worship and fast rather than to hold a committee meeting. It was in this context that God revealed his purpose for Barnabas and Saul. We see no lengthy or complicated selection process here. God spoke, and they listened, obeyed, and continued in fasting and prayer.

While I am not advocating that we remove all of our current processes and systems, I do think this season of uncertainty and change calls for more worship, prayer, and fasting, and less clinging to processes that may not be as effective as they once were. In Acts 14:23, we witness the importance of prayer and fasting once again. Here Paul and Barnabas identify elders for the new churches they were mentoring. "Paul and Barnabas appointed elders for them in each church and, with prayer and fasting, committed them to the Lord, in whom they had put their trust." These New Testament leaders sought the Lord's direction, facilitated what he directed, and committed the work into his hands. In those early days of the church, they relied much more on the guidance of the Holy Spirit than on firmly established processes, lengthy committee meetings, and consensus through voting.

I believe God can use this current season of shaking and shifting to draw us back to a deeper dependence on the Holy Spirit. Jesus' promise in John 16 echoes strongly through the centuries holding rich hope for us today! As we encounter the challenges of our own day, Jesus promises us a Helper to guide us in all decisions and walk beside us as we grow in using the gifts he releases in our lives. When we rely on the revelation of his truth, we can expect to see God move in powerful ways! This season of shaking will reveal the glory of God's unshakable kingdom to which we belong.

Reflections and Applications

What is my natural style of leadership? Do I lead like a chess master or a gardener? What has contributed to my leadership style? How can I grow as a leader in this season?

What are my ministry/spiritual gifts? How am I using them today? How can I help others develop in their gifts?

NOTES

1. Stanley McChrystal, *Team of Teams: New Rules of Engagement for a Complex World* (New York: Penguin Publishing Group, 2015), 231.
2. Stanley McChrystal, *Team of Teams*, 128.
3. Stanley McChrystal, *Team of Teams*, 225.
4. Romans 12; I Corinthians 1
5. Acts 13:1

CHAPTER 16
A TIME OF SHAKING

Since we are receiving a Kingdom that is unshakable, let us be thankful.
—Hebrews 12:28 NLT

While working in student development at a Christian
university, I witnessed how critical the college years are
in the formation of identity, worldview, and values.
Many students arrive on campus from a somewhat closed
environment. The beliefs and views of their parents,
teachers, church, and social networks influence their
perspectives and often limit their understanding of the
world. College gives students an opportunity to interact
with people from diverse places, divergent backgrounds,
and contrary worldviews. As their understanding of
the world expands, they may be forced to wrestle with
questions regarding what they believe and why they
believe it. If navigated well with the support of parents,
good friends, and wise counselors, this process is
incredibly powerful. Students learn how to identify the
values and views of their families of origin as well as what
they were taught in their earlier education as it relates

to the larger world. The result is a worldview that has been tested and defined—one that will guide them more effectively as they move into adulthood.

During cultural shifts, all of us experience elements of the college student experience as our worldviews are challenged by emerging views. The result may be disconcerting to us as long-held perspectives and processes come under scrutiny. The perceptions of those grounded in modern views sometimes clash with emerging trends. This clash, however, presents a valuable opportunity to wrestle with and weigh the validity, effectiveness, and truth of diverse perspectives. It allows us to identify which of our values are biblical and which are cultural. As we do so, a renewed commitment to biblical principles can emerge. I call this a time of shaking.

The Shaking

A variety of factors are contributing to the current shaking taking place in our society. As previously mentioned, one is society's changing values as we move from the Modern Era to a new era. Another is that America is the most diverse country ever to exist. There are no road maps for navigating the range of customs, beliefs, traditions, and perspectives that represent our nation. Throughout history and around the world today, diversity continues to result in genocides, slavery, war, and the oppression, expulsion, or isolation of certain groups. America has always been a grand experiment—one that continues today as we navigate the imperfect and messy process of understanding what it means to thrive as a united nation.

Added to the changing values and complexities of society is the fact that technology provides a platform for all views to be promoted, discussed, and analyzed by anyone, anywhere, anytime. In the past couple of decades, the closed environments of local communities, families, churches, and even regions have given way to an increasing scope of perspectives and opinions. Author Dan Levitan explains, "In 2011, Americans took in five times as much information every day as they did in 1986."[1] That number continues to increase. Recent reports estimate more data has been created in the past two years than in the entire previous history of humanity.[2] Access to ideas and data today is unprecedented. Sifting through and making sense of all the information coming at us constantly can be overwhelming.

An additional factor contributing to the shaking of our society is globalization. We live in a time when the actions and decisions of one nation significantly affect others around the world. Furthermore, modern technology gives us front row seats to witness the injustices, disasters, heartache, and pain of a global community on a daily basis. The human psyche was not designed to absorb and manage the pain of millions of people. We often struggle just to manage our own. Still, we are forced to address issues previously ignored or denied while confronting ideas that were once distant or vague. Doing so requires us to revisit our motives, values, and convictions, and examine our hearts.

Seeking the Unshakable

More than a decade ago, I heard a sermon series based on Hebrews 12:25-28. The theme was the unshakable kingdom. I have since come to see that message as a prophetic one for us today. The passage reads,

> See to it that you do not refuse him who speaks. If they did not escape when they refused him who warned them on earth, how much less will we, if we turn away from him who warns us from heaven? At that time his voice shook the earth, but now he has promised, "Once more I will shake not only the earth but also the heavens." The words "once more" indicate the removing of what can be shaken—that is, created things—so that what cannot be shaken may remain. Therefore, since we are receiving a kingdom that cannot be shaken, let us be thankful, and so worship God acceptably with reverence and awe.

This passage of Scripture references the physical shaking that occurred when God descended on Mount Sinai to meet with Moses in Exodus 19. Hebrews 12, however, refers to another shaking that will remove what can be shaken so that what cannot be shaken—what belongs to His unshakable kingdom—will remain.

As Individuals

This shaking is taking place on several levels today. On an individual level, we find that we can no longer blend into our culture and remain faithful to God's truth at the same time. We live in an environment that is increasingly hostile toward God as it declares truth to be relative or altogether irrelevant.[3] In previous seasons, many considered Christianity to be culturally acceptable. In some places like the Bible Belt, communities revolved around the local church. We expected individuals running for political office to attend a church. Many businesses also acknowledged Christian holidays. Unfortunately, not all cultural Christians lived as devoted followers of Christ.

As cultural Christianity fades, we face a decision. Will we look like the culture around us? Or like Daniel, will we continue to pray when it is prohibited, in some cases risking our reputations, comforts, and even our lives? Such shaking requires intentionality in our convictions. We must decide on what and on whom we will base our lives. Will we live according to God's Word, or the cultural norms and expectations around us?

In Politics and Society

For believers, this shaking is also playing out in communities, politics, and churches. Because I speak on cultural and generational issues in our increasingly divided society, I am often asked politically-charged questions. This is what I have observed. Many American Christians choose to be American first and Christian second. As they engage both believers and unbelievers, they prioritize their political and social views rather than biblical truths. I find this to be the case on both sides of the aisle. Don't get me wrong. Politics are important, but faith is more important.

Both history and Scripture show that governments and nations are merely temporary and cannot last forever. If we make our political or social views more important than obedience to God's Word, we prioritize something that is fading away. Many claim to be Christians, yet they allow their views to make them hateful and angry toward others. First John 2:9 clearly states, "Anyone who claims to be in the light but hates a brother or sister is still in the darkness." Current social and political divisions and upheavals reveal where we have prioritized those things that can be shaken over those that cannot.

As individuals, communities, and families, we have an opportunity to examine and realign our hearts, motives, and perspectives according to biblical priorities. Daniel served under several kings and two empires. His dedication to remain the person God called him to be and to rely on the unshakable truths of God allowed him to survive and thrive as kings and kingdoms rose and fell around him. He set his hope on the permanence of the only kingdom that will not and cannot be shaken. As godly leaders in the tumultuous environment of today, this must be our approach as well. Our hope rests in a kingdom that outlasts every social movement, political party, military endeavor, and earthly leader!

In the Church

Today's church can be shaken as well, especially as it relates to intergenerational differences. While generational views traditionally differ with reference to cosmetic elements such as style of music, type of programs, décor, etc., these differences are intensified by the clash of foundational values. Diverse perspectives on truth, sexuality, gender, politics, and race collide and produce resentment, division, and confusion.

The influence of the Modern Era permeated much of traditional church culture. We evangelized and promoted biblical validity using facts, logic, and science. We often measured success by budgets, bodies, and buildings rather than spiritual health and growth. We built organizational structures that relied on a few to do the ministry of many. Even so, God has worked in and through this imperfect culture and the heart and efforts of his modern body of believers. The questioning of postmodern natives, however, prompts us to consider what elements of our faith practices are more culturally based versus those that are more biblically based. Engaging this discussion will make it possible to shake off what can be shaken in order to refocus on those beliefs and practices that cannot be shaken.

This season of the church calls for honest, loving, and committed conversation between all generations. If young believers insist on forming their own churches or faith gatherings and fail to converse with those they perceive to be closeminded or outdated, they risk developing a church burdened with the shakable elements of the emerging culture. Likewise, if older members refuse to engage the questions and concerns of younger ones, their views face certain extinction along with the death of the Modern Era. This unique moment in history offers a chance for those holding different cultural values to come together. If we can be believers first and part of our culture second, then intergenerational churches will be free to focus on powerful shared biblical truths while encouraging one another to serve in an ungodly culture. This is a truly powerful, and I believe, critical element of what God longs to do among us today.

Receiving the Unshakable Kingdom

Today, God calls us to choose—not refuse—his kingdom, his promises, his truth. This is a kingdom that cannot be shaken even when the world, culture, society, and circumstances around us reflect chaos and upheaval. Those who hold tightly to God in this tumultuous season have a hope that cannot be overwhelmed. The world desperately needs this kind of hope. However, it will not be the masses that understand and respond to this hope, but rather the faithful remnant. These are the leaders God will use, as he did Daniel and his friends, to make his glory known before kings and throughout ungodly kingdoms and cultures!

Reflections and Applications

What issues or topics cause you to feel angry, frustrated, or bitter toward other believers? Are there values or issues you prioritize over God's truth and love in your life?

How are you engaging with believers from other generations? Are you actively listening and trying to learn from them? How could you do this more effectively?

NOTES

1. Daniel J. Levitin, *The Organized Mind: Thinking Straight in the Age of Information Overload* (New York: Penguin, 2014), 6.

2. Bernard Marr, "Big Data: 20 Mind-Boggling Facts Everyone Must Read," *Forbes*, posted September 30, 2015, https://www.forbes.com/sites/bernardmarr/2015/09/30/big-data-20-mind-boggling-facts-everyone-must-read/#456ceeec17b1.

3. "Word of the Year," *Oxford English Dictionaries*, accessed February 3, 2018, https://en.oxforddictionaries.com/word-of-the-year/word-of-the-year-2016.

CHAPTER 17
A SEASON OF A REMNANT

But the Lord said to Gideon, "There are still too many men. Take them down to the water, and I will thin them out for you there."

—Judges 7:4

Our culture obsesses over numbers. We quantify success as the number of clients or sales, miles run, or likes on social media. Our sense of worth is often linked to our GPA, paycheck, or retirement portfolio. The urgency to measure success even infiltrates the church. While there are some great reasons for measuring, it can also be a distraction. Scripture shows us again and again that God does not measure success in numbers. If anything, the opposite is true. God receives great glory when he uses the one or the few and the most unlikely!

Focusing on the Few

In his book, *Radical*, David Platt describes a powerful consideration for us when developing leaders for the future: "My model in ministry is a guy who spent the majority of his ministry time with twelve men. A guy who, when he left this earth, had only about 120 people who were actually sticking around and doing what he told them to do."[1] Based on those numbers, most American churches would not deem Jesus' ministry very successful. Scripture gives no indication that God obsesses over numbers the way we do. In fact, he has demonstrated again and again that he shows his power through the few, a remnant. In the case of Babylon, God used four young men to touch the hearts of kings. In Gideon's day, he downsized an army. In the first century, he used a faithful 120 to spread his message to the world.

Truly embracing the God who does not define success in numbers may require a redefining of priorities for the American church. It might be painful as positions are redefined, programs reconsidered, and ministry goals reevaluated, but I believe this is part of the shaking. A time and place exist for large-scale ministry such as the feeding of the 5,000 in Matthew 14, or the conversion of the 3,000 in Acts 2, but we live in a time when we must focus on a remnant. The American church has been so caught up in numbers that we have, at times, neglected the few. The emerging season of ministry is about focusing more on a remnant rather than on the masses. The changes in our culture, as well as the perspectives, needs, and desires of young leaders are driving forces behind this shift.

Interpretation vs. Information

So, what is our focus if not numbers? Today, we access information unlike any other generation in the history of the world. We don't need another great program to give us information. We need to process the information we have. Generational expert Tim Elmore explains, "Students today need teachers more for interpretation than information."[2] Interactions with trusted colleagues, mentors, and friends can provide valuable insight and opportunities for thinking, understanding, and developing our values and convictions. Relationships, godly community, and spirit-led conversation and experiences provide the most formative lessons. Our task to equip the leaders of the future echoes Jesus' ministry to his disciples and those closest to him. After he died, rose, and returned to heaven, it was this remnant that met in the upper room and then carried forth his ministry.

I am often asked how to create a successful leadership development or ministry program for youth or young adults. Large-scale methods are rarely effective. The best way to engage with and develop a young person is one-on-one and in small teams or communities. God working in and through our lives provides the ideal curriculum to use in preparing leaders who want God to lead them. The ability to be vulnerable and honest about our mistakes, weaknesses, joys, and hopes, when coupled with God's faithfulness in our lives, will inspire other leaders to trust in our sovereign Father regardless of what individual seasons of leadership might hold. Methods may vary, but faith in God is the source of our inspiration. This is the message we must share with the remnant God places in our lives.

Ministry to the one or the few requires time, patience, and the giving of oneself. It is easy to measure progress when we plan an event, check items off a list, follow the points in a Bible study, or deliver a well-crafted sermon. When we sit with people as they process what biblical truth looks like in a complicated situation, model the graceful handling of a leadership mistake, or speak truth in love, success is often hard to determine. This season of equipping a remnant requires sacrificial intergenerational relationships in which we share perspectives, experiences, and questions. When we fully engage in such conversations, we will discover the wisdom we need to redefine leadership and humble service to one another. In this way, we actively demonstrate the love of God in and through our lives!

Key Qualities of a Mentor

I thoroughly enjoyed watching *The Intern*, a movie starring Robert De Niro and Anne Hathaway. It beautifully depicts the value and necessity of intergenerational relationships and why we desperately need older leaders and mentors to remain engaged as young leaders seek the wisdom of experience. Hathaway plays the role of a young, highly successful Millennial entrepreneur who struggles to find balance between her demanding, evolving professional career and her young family. De Niro, a widower, is a retired professional whose former job in the printing industry has become obsolete. As a retiree, he does it all. He learns Mandarin, tries yoga, and travels extensively. Still, he is dissatisfied with his lifestyle and applies for an internship at Hathaway's company.

As an older intern working for a Millennial entrepreneur, De Niro's character is representative of what mature, wise, and sacrificial leaders offer future generations. First, he shows up for work on time each and every day. Ignored by his Millennial boss at first, he spends most of his days sitting in front of a computer with nothing to do. Unused to being idle, he engages the young interns to his right and left. He makes an effort to know the employees, helps with random tasks, and becomes the person everyone can count on. He comes to work each day in a tailored suit and carries his old-school briefcase. His calm and thoughtful presence quickly becomes a gift to the young, frazzled professionals around him.

Second, the character De Niro plays is observant. Years spent as a professional have taught him to notice and appreciate skills and dynamics often lost on younger people. As a result, he asks questions, provides assistance, and gives counsel and affirmation his younger colleagues desperately need. His input changes the lives of those he interacts with on a daily basis.

Third, he is patient. Even though the young people around him often fail to acknowledge his contribution and wisdom, he remains consistent, patiently doing his work and just being himself. Eventually, his boss asks him for help and advice, and fellow employees recognize and celebrate his significant contributions. As a result of his presence and influence, the organizational culture changes, and his fellow interns even begin to wear suits and buy briefcases! In short, he earns the right to be heard, followed, and imitated. His example and presence prove influential to young professionals who are learning and forming habits that will follow them the rest of their careers.

Today, as we prepare a remnant of godly leaders to serve God, we need mentors who will actively engage in modeling servant leadership to those around them. We also need young leaders who will humbly seek and learn from the wisdom of seasoned leaders God brings into their lives.

Investing in a Remnant

Our essential task in this season consists of praying for, teaching, loving, and being the remnant that will lead in the days ahead. What happens if we fail to invest in ministry to a remnant? We discussed in previous chapters the trends in our culture and their impact on young people. The ranks of those with deep conviction and sincere faith in God seem dismally small. If we fail to intentionally engage in mentoring, developing, and equipping a strong remnant, we may very well witness the rise of a generation like the one described in Judges 2. After the generation of the godly leader, Joshua, passed away, it was replaced by those who did not know God or what he had done. While Joshua's generation believed in and served God, they failed to plant the seeds of faith in the next generation. The same must not be said of our time.

So, who is your remnant? Where are the young people and leaders who represent the seed of what God will do in the future? Look around your church, your family, or your community. Who are the young people who are already there? You don't need to go out and find them. You just need to engage them! Invite them to coffee, ask if you can babysit their kids, help them with a school project, or ask them how you can support a dream or ministry idea they have. Is there a young leader in your business? Maybe you have noticed a neighbor kid who is going through a tough time or a young professional who might benefit from an experienced intern helping her out? Engaging a remnant does not necessarily mean abandoning other approaches to ministry. However, I do think that by intentionally investing our time and energy in a few younger people, we are able to encourage deep spiritual growth and preparation for the future. Regardless, I believe there is a call for a general shift in the American church away from success measured in numbers to ministry success measured in the effective equipping of disciples, especially those who will be godly leaders in the decades to come.

The Remnant in Babylon

The Babylonian culture in which Daniel and his friends found themselves demanded utmost obedience to the king. It took conviction, courage, and faith to stand firm in their devotion to God. It is unlikely that their leaders or mentors back in Judah encountered the complex choices these young men faced in Nebuchadnezzar's palace. By studying Judah's history, though, we see how God used godly leaders like King Josiah and the prophet Jeremiah to ensure that a seed of faith was planted in these young men's lives. As a result, even before entering Babylon, they already knew their God and understood his ways. They carried their faith with them into Babylon. The same God who allowed Nebuchadnezzar to destroy the temple showed up repeatedly in defense of those who were faithful to him in an ungodly culture.

In the days ahead, Christian leaders may feel discouraged as some churches and faith-based organizations close their doors, as the number of those claiming to be Christians decreases in our country, and as religious freedoms and biblical values come increasingly under attack. However, God is raising up a remnant, a Daniel Generation. God is calling on experienced leaders to humbly and sacrificially plant the seed of faith in the heart of the next generation. He is calling a generation of young men and women to stand firm under incredible pressure from an ungodly culture. We must know how to refuse the defiled food, pray three times a day, and stand when all others bow to the statue of gold. God will be with us whether in a king's palace or a lion's den. As we are faithful to him, we will see his power displayed and his name glorified in miraculous ways. We will have the honor of being faithful to our unchanging God in a season of great change. We will be the Daniel Generation.

Reflections and Applications

How do I measure success in my life and ministry? Does my definition of success differ from God's?

Who is my remnant? Who are the leaders and individuals God has placed in my life for me to encourage? How could I do this better?

NOTES

1. David Platt, *Radical: Taking Back Your Faith from the American Dream*, (Colorado Springs: Multnomah Books, 2010), 1-2.

2. Tim Elmore, Twitter post, February 3, 2018, 6:35 a.m., https://twitter.com/TimElmore/status/959749577082589184.

Resource List

Chapter 2

- *A Primer on Postmodernism* by Stanley J. Grenz
- *Marching Off the Map: Inspire Students to Navigate a Brand New World* by Tim Elmore
- *Post-Capitalist Society* by Peter Drucker
- *Postmodern Pilgrims: First Century Passion for the 21ˢᵗ Century World* by Leonard Sweet
- *The Beauty of Intolerance* by Josh McDowell and Sean McDowell
- *The Great Emergence: How Christianity is Changing and Why* by Phyllis Tickle
- *The Shallows: What the Internet is Doing to Our Brain* by Nicholas Carr

Chapter 9

- *7 Basic Steps to Successful Fasting and Prayer* by Dr. Bill Bright, (https://www.cru.org/us/en/train-and-grow/spiritual-growth/fasting/7-steps-to-fasting.html)
- *Celebration of Discipline: The Path to Spiritual Growth* by Richard J. Foster
- *Shaping History Through Prayer and Fasting* by Derek Prince

Chapter 10

- *Emotional Intelligence 2.0* by Terry Bradberry and Jean Greaves
- *Emotional Intelligence: Why It Can Matter More Than IQ* by Daniel Goleman

Chapter 15

- *Accelerate: Building Strategic Agility for a Faster-Moving World* by John Kotter
- *Catch the Wind of the Spirit: How the Five Ministry Gifts Can Transform Your Church* by Carolyn Tennant
- IPSAT Leadership Coaching (http://myipsat.com/coach/jolene-erlacher)
- IPSAT Small Group Experience (https://www.leadingtomorrow.org/leadership-coaching.html)
- *Leadership Eat Last: Why Some Teams Pull Together and Others Don't* by Simon Sinek
- Spiritual Gifts Assessment (www.spiritualgiftstest.com)
- *Team of Teams: New Rules of Engagement for a Complex World* by General Stanley McChrystal and Tatum Collins
- *The Five Dysfunctions of a Team: A Leadership Fable* by Patrick Lencioni
- *The Five Dysfunctions of a Team: A Field Guide* by Patrick Lencioni

Glossary of Terms

Baby Boomers: people who were born between 1946-1964.

Digital Native: a person born or raised during the age of digital technology and familiar with technological devices and the internet from an early age.

Generation X: people who were born between 1965-1979.

Generation Z: people who were born between 1996-2012.

Millennial Generation: people who were born between 1980-1995.

Modern Era: a period of history that began with the European Renaissance (about 1420-1630) and marked a transition out of the Middle Ages. The Modern period is associated with individualism, capitalism, urbanization, and globalization. It was an era that began with the invention of the printing press and was marked by significant developments in science, politics, warfare, and technology.

Moral Relativism: the position that moral or ethical

standards do not reflect objective or universal moral truths, but instead are relative to social, cultural, historical, or personal circumstances and preferences.

Silent Generation: people who were born between 1925-1945.

Postmodernism: a reaction to the modern mindset that assumed certainty of scientific, or objective, efforts to explain reality. Postmodernism is skeptical of explanations which claim to be valid for all groups, cultures, and races, and instead, focuses on the relative truths of each individual's experience.

Postmodern Natives: people who were raised and educated in a culture or environment that embraces and teaches postmodern values and perspectives.

ABOUT THE AUTHOR
JOLENE CASSELLIUS ERLACHER

Jolene grew up as a missionary kid in Latin America, where she learned how culture influences our worldview and faith. Later, while working on staff at a Christian university, she studied the impact of generational and cultural trends in churches and workplaces. This led to her first book, *Millennials in Ministry* (Judson Press), which discusses the values of young leaders in the church and ministry contexts.

Jolene is also the author of *Daniel Generation: Godly Leadership in an Ungodly Culture*. As a mother, teacher, and mentor, Jolene is passionate about discipling and equipping the next generation to thrive as godly leaders in our complex world. She believes God is uniquely equipping Millennials and Generation Z believers to be the leaders our world needs today.

An adjunct professor, Jolene teaches graduate courses on organizational leadership and generational trends. She also speaks and consults extensively on understanding today's students, kids and technology, intergenerational leadership and ministry, and equipping the next generation of leaders.

Connect with Jolene

Website: www.leadingtomorrow.org
Email: jolene@leadingtomorrow.org
Facebook: www.facebook.com/danielgeneration
Twitter: @joleneerlacher
Instagram: @danielgenerationbook

Book Jolene to Speak

Schedule Jolene to speak to your group
or at your next event:

info@leadingtomorrow.org